The Little Bear Story

Story

The Adventures of a Retarded Gopher Skinner

Autobiography
of
Evangelist
Richard "Little Bear" Wheeler

Published By
Mantle Ministries: 228 Still Ridge
Bulverde, Texas 78163
http://www.mantlemin.com or e-mail mantle3377@aol.com

Special thanks for
Cover design:
Al Mendenhall Graphics
Cover photos:
The Jackson Ranch-Stonewall, Texas

CONTENTS

Preface

It seems a bit strange for someone who is only forty-nine to consider doing an autobiography before time has ebbed the hour glass of one's life nearly away. There were several concerns I had in attempting this project. The first and foremost was that I feared that those readers beyond my immediate family would think I was egotistical. Secondly, I was concerned this work would be a complete waste of my limited time, for who would even care to read such a personal record of an insignificant, small-time evangelist. All of the above arguments were dispelled as I began to ponder what would be my real intent in writing my life story. I concluded, as you will see for yourself, that my motivation would be first for my family, as a legacy of what the Lord has done on my behalf, however brief my sojourn here on earth. I realized that if I waited to write down the deeds of my life until a future time, how could I be reassured that I would have a future to write, since as the Bible declares *"our life is but a vapor" (James 4:14).*

I can now say, two years later, after the book is finished that whether my family, personal friends, and ministry friends will ever read this or not, I do not regret one iota having accomplished this task for the time being. As I began to write, it was necessary to force myself to mentally slow down long enough to retrace the paths I had traveled while here on earth. As I did, I discovered a most wonderful experience. I realized that my life has been directed by the hand of God since birth. I was able to retrace the events that led to my salvation, and the pain-staking events that God used to lead me to Himself. I, once again, relived the marriage to my wonderful wife Marilyn, and experienced anew the birth of my children, and the joy that it had brought to my former days. What joy and assurance of the love of Christ toward me.

This writing has strengthened my faith and confidence in that *"He which hath begun a good work in you will perform it until the day of Jesus Christ" (Phil 1:6)*.

I can now confidently challenge you to discipline your time in such a way so that you can begin to record all the Lord has done in your life. You will be amazed how slowing down long enough to reflect and write of those timely events in your days is good medicine to your bones. Your story is most significant to your immediate family, if not to the general public, and they stand to lose the heritage God has done in and through you on His behalf. It is a tragedy that people die and leave no record of their lives. Can you imagine what it would have been like if the Apostles Paul, Peter, John, historical characters like, Washington, Jefferson, Franklin, and a multitude of other known and relatively obscure people had not written of their life experiences. We would have been robbed of giving glory to God for the deeds He has done through them.

I beseech you earnestly to record your story before it is too late. All testimonies, however slight to the person are of great value, and in heaven there will not be one who boasts that their life was more worthy than another, for all will see that they played important parts in the drama of life.

CHAPTER 1

The Beginnings

I wish, like Davy Crockett, that I could say, *"I was born on the mountain tops of Tennessee."* However, the Lord saw fit to bring me forth in the "City of Angels," Los Angeles, California. I was delivered on November 24, 1948, at Queen of Angels Hospital. Upon my arrival, I already had a sister who was nearly two years old. Her name was Sylvia. For you, the reader, I believe it is important to give a brief sketch of my family history so as to enable you to better understand my life story. This is especially so since my mother and father have an out-of-the-ordinary story.

My maternal grandfather, of Spanish decent, worked for the Mexican government, and it was the nature of his job to be working out of both New York and Mexico City; thus, he had two places of residence with Mexican citizenship. On May 1, 1921, while he and my grandmother, of Irish decent, were in New York my mother, Elizabeth May Artigas, was born. Elizabeth's mother died by the time Elizabeth was three years old ,and, through a series of events, she was placed in a convent with the Carmelite order of nuns in Mexico City. There, she attended school and had very little contact with her father and family. By the time she was eighteen years of age, Elizabeth made the decision to take her first vows to become a Carmelite nun. In some ways, my mother's story is similar to that of Maria Von Trapp's as told in the famed movie *The Sound of Music*.

Over a period of time, as a nun on her "novice" vows, my mother worked in various types of ministry. She soon concluded that life as a nun was not her true calling, so she left the Carmelite order. After securing a few different jobs to help support herself, she met and became enamored with a certain young man. They courted briefly until she discovered that he was already married and was planning to divorce his current wife. My mother was embarrassed and mortified when she heard the news, and so she decided to flee to Los Angeles, California. She obtained the necessary legal papers and acquired a small flat in downtown Los Angeles where she found herself looking for work.

Within a short period of time, my mother met a Mexican-born, naturalized citizen who was bilingual named Richard Basil Lobato. Out of desperation and fear of being destitute in a new country, my mother befriended Richard Lobato—a man at least fifteen years her senior. Perhaps aflame because of her insecurities and fears, a romantic relationship soon developed and my mother practically proposed to Mr. Lobato who was destined to become my father.

My sister Sylvia was born on February 7, 1947. Almost two years later, I was conceived. When my father learned of the news that Elizabeth was with child again, he suggested that she terminate the pregnancy because he didn't want to assume responsibility for another child. Praise be to God, my mother's convictions empowered her to insist that it would be a sin and, she refused to interfere with God's creation. She won the victory, and I was born.

I do not consider myself to be a particularly special person. However, I can humbly say that if I had not been born, I could hardly imagine what it would be like not to have had the joy and privilege of being married to my lovely wife, Marilyn, and having our three precious children. There would not be the ministry over which God has so graciously given me a stewardship which has affected thousands of people across the United States of America, Canada, and Mexico.

Sometimes I think about my beginnings and can only imagine what would and would not have been had I been aborted. Only eternity can decipher the works and blessings of God that have been unfulfilled by the abortion of a child.

CHAPTER 2

Early Years

One morning when I was about five years old, my mother received a surprise when someone knocked on the door of our home. Mother opened the door to find a Hispanic woman close to her own age who said, "I am looking for my husband, Richard Lobato."

Of course, my mother asked the woman, "What are you talking about?"

The woman assured my mother that she had not come to cause any trouble. She only wanted Richard to sign some legal papers.

When my father came home that day, my mother told him about the surprise visitor. Quite casually, my father responded, "Oh, that was my wife to whom I am still married. She probably wants me to sign divorce papers. You asked me to marry you, and I didn't want to pass up such a great opportunity, so I left her and married you."

The upshot of all this is that my mother was a nun, my father was a bigamist, and I turned out to be an evangelist! You can only surmise that my life story will be just as peculiar.

Between the ages of five and seven, no significant event occurred-except for one that left an indelible impression in my storehouse of memories. One summer, while my family was vacationing in Mexico, my father pulled our 1952 Buick Sedan into a gas station. He told me to stay in the car while he pumped the gas. At about that moment, I looked to my left and saw a squad of Mexican foot soldiers marching on a bridge. I decided to sneak out of the car so I could get a better view of what I considered to be a most wonderful attraction. They even had rifles and spit-n-polish uniforms. After a short march across the bridge, the soldiers disappeared from sight, so I swiftly re-entered the car without anyone noticing and took special care to close the car door without making a noise.

Shortly afterward, my dad pulled out of the gas station and drove back onto the bumpy Mexican highway. As he gained speed and was approaching a tight left-hand curve, my small-framed body was pressed against the back seat passenger door. I soon learned that while I had successfully deceived my parents, I had failed to securely close the door. At the precise moment that we took the sharp curve, the door flew open and I went hurling out. I found myself flying through the air like Superman. It was exhilarating until I realized that my mortal body, unlike Superman's body of steel, was going to make a crash landing.

The landing was so forceful that I found myself pitched toward a very steep desert ravine full of cacti and other prickly growth indigenous to the region. Surely, this was the end of my very short life—or so I thought. Suddenly, out of nowhere and at just the right moment, a hand grabbed me. The precious hand of my mother reached out and rescued me. Only God knows how and from where she came. Mothers always have a way of rescuing their children, even naughty disobedient ones, just as our Heavenly Father rescues His wayward children who call upon Him as Lord to be their Rescuer and Savior.

I returned to the car to lick my wounds. In my heart I repented for my disobedience in leaving the car at the gas station. *"Now no chastening for the present seemeth to be joyous, but grievous: nevertheless afterward it yieldeth the peaceable fruit of righteousness unto them which are exercised [trained] thereby"* (Hebrews 12:11).

Life has many lessons to offer if only we accept them. If, as Christians, we choose to obey our Heavenly Father and His Word, we remain safe in the protection of His car of love as we speed and turn down the highways of life. If, on the other hand, we choose to disobey Him, we place ourselves in a car of danger bound to pitch us out into the storms of life where prickly cacti and deep ravines await the opportunity to afflict us. Our Heavenly Father is faithful to chasten us so that we may return under His wing of protection and blessing. *"Before I was afflicted I went astray: but now have I kept thy word . . . It is good for me that I have been afflicted; that I might learn thy statutes . . . I know, O LORD, that thy judgments are right, and that thou in faithfulness hast afflicted me"* (Psalm 119:67, 71, and 75). It is possible that the car of danger may even drive us to our death as a result of our rebellion and disobedience. Praise the Lord for His goodness and mercy! I received only minor injuries, a few bumps and bruises. Even my mother, who had jumped out to rescue me from the moving car, was kept from harm.

As I look back over my early home life, I recall being timid around my father because he seemed very nervous. He did not seem to have the patience that was required to train and raise Sylvia and me along with his two other children (Susanna and George) from his previous marriage. He would hit me on the head over minor infractions. Thus, whenever he would pass behind or near me, I would flinch, as I was afraid he would give me another knuckle buster.

Since I was born into a Latin family with a mother who was a former nun, I was raised a Roman Catholic. I attended the neighborhood Catholic school and completed kindergarten in full graduation regalia. Meanwhile, back at home, my mother was a devoted housewife who tended to all our needs and sometimes our wants. She later told me that she never really appreciated my father or loved him greatly because he was so much older than she and that she married him out of necessity. My father, on the other hand, worshiped my mother and showered her with the kind of love and affection which most wives would cherish. However, my mother was spoiled and immature—two traits which do not contribute to the making of a good marriage.

My mother tells me that upon my father's return home from work each day, he would follow her around the house and insist that she be within his sight at all times. His behavior became obsessive and was an annoyance to my mother. Once, to get away from him for a moment, she ducked into the bedroom and locked the door. However, this did not deter my father. He simply went outside to stare at her from the bedroom window. My mother thought this was so funny that she broke into laughter and allowed my father back into her presence.

Another story my mother tells is about the time she awoke from a deep sleep with a feeling of something being wrong. Upon opening her eyes, she found my father wide-awake in the wee hours of the morning staring at her, because he was so awed by her beauty. My mother hit him with a pillow and told him to go to sleep. He was so embarrassed he complied.

During family gatherings, my father was the life of the party. He had a good sense of humor and was loved by all. However, despite being a hard worker and provider, it seems my father had some emotional problems. In August of 1955, my father complained that he was tired—

something he never did. He was also very despondent over the fact that my mother and he had been in a marital argument a day or so before. I remember that morning vividly. I entered my father's bedroom and found him dead on the bed. An ambulance came and took him away. To this day, my mother has never told me the truth about his death, but relatives say he died of a drug overdose. If he was addicted to drugs, it could perhaps explain why he seemed so nervous and why his behavior toward my mother seemed obsessive and abnormal.

It is sad to say, but as a fatherless seven-year-old boy, I really did not miss my father. Perhaps my memory of those early years is clouded for the purpose of self-preservation and my father's absence relieved my fear of him. I can't say that I ever felt loved by him nor did I ever get to really know him or grow to love him myself.

CHAPTER 3

Early Schooling

My early school years were like being in the military. In those days, the Roman Catholic schools were rough places where "Sisters" surely learned their teaching methods from military drill sergeants. These Sisters looked like Darth Vader in *Star Wars* before the movie was ever thought of. The most feared and dreaded Sister was Sister Superior. I could hardly discern their faces since they were covered with a huge black and white starched shroud. This was very intimidating to a little first grader. From what I've been told, I was definitely a handful, even for those Sisters who were trained to combat and deal with problem children. They had to bring out their entire arsenal of dastardly tools to shape, mold, and break the wild stallion in my undisciplined nature.

We didn't have fancy medical terms that labeled dysfunctional children in those days. I am convinced that it was because of my behavior that medical science invented terms like hyperactive, attention deficit disorder, and dyslexia, as well as the drug Ritalin to sedate children. I still have my elementary Catholic school report cards with horrible grades and notes written on the back informing my mother that I was "retarded." This caused my mother to take me to the family doctor so he could tell her what to do with her "retarded" son. The doctor psychoanalyzed me and declared to my mother that I was a "normal" child. He further related his suspicion that perhaps *she* was the one with brain damage since *she* had brought me to see him for *my* "retardation." Needless to say, we were both relieved to find out that we were sane. Note that we were "sane" but not necessarily "normal" individuals.

Meanwhile back at boot camp—err, I mean school– the Sisters were literally going to knock some sense into me even if it killed one of us. Today, the Children's Social Services Division would have had those teachers arrested for the things they put me through. I can personally testify that our ears cannot be pulled off! What I considered to be my best behavior was *most intolerable* to the Sisters.

The Sisters had learned maneuvers in holy boot camp—such as sneaking up behind my desk and grabbing my ears as if they were handles and pulling me up to the front of the class. Next, they would twist my ear to a point that would drive me to my knees, which they believed would bring me to sorrow and repentance. However, at seven years of age, it only brought me to pain, humility, and fear. After a few minutes of this, I was lifted by my armpits and given a good shaking accompanied by a hell-fire and brimstone lecture. All this came with that huge shroud looking into my face. Goliath couldn't have looked any more ferocious at that moment. Then the *coup de grace* began when my arms and hands were forced to be fully extended so that the oak chalkboard pointer could be lifted by the Sister to full height and brought down upon the top of my hands in full execution style. I was then sent back to my desk to hang my head in shame and wonder what was wrong with me. In my mind, as well as my mother's and the doctor's, I was perfectly normal. I guess I was just too "retarded" to consider that something was wrong with *me*.

My older sister and teachers who happened to have been born with "brains" constantly reminded me that I was stupid. Bless their hearts, these Sisters tried to put the fear of God into me so that I would shape up.

I flunked first grade and received many lectures on the dangers of hell and how "bad little boys" like me would go there if they didn't behave themselves. I was told to go to confession as soon as possible and to make sure that I didn't get hit by a car on the way or I would go to purgatory for eons of time or, worse yet, end up in the place of eternal torment. I took all these things very seriously. Even as a teen, I remember always crossing the street on my way to confession with extreme caution so that I wouldn't get hit by a car and end up going to hell.

The impressions left on me by these Sisters have *never completely* been erased from my mind. By the time I was in the fourth grade, I had received enough catechism to make me a priest, which I seriously considered as a vocation because I had a deep love for the Savior Jesus Christ. By the time I was eight years old, I must have been a real loser, because my relatives could hardly tolerate being around me and my overactive nature.

I finally latched onto something that became meaningful to me. A "bug bit me"—a life-changing bug. It bit many a child back in the 1950s. Yep, the bug was the "Crockett bug." The actor, Fess Parker, who portrayed Davy Crockett, captured the wild imagination of boys such as myself. Since most mountain men lacked schooling and were probably a bit "touched in the head" like me, I figured that I could be just like Davy Crockett. Discovering Davy gave me something that I could finally relate to. The only problem was that there was not a single beaver for me to trap in all of Los Angeles, so I was a bit frustrated.

However, I could and did spend my days fantasizing my role and pretending to be a mountain man. I dreamed of a time when I could get a real rifle for myself and become a trapper. That dream was on the horizon, and it came in the form of a new dad.

CHAPTER 4

A New Dad

A major turning point in my life occurred when I was eight years old. My mother found Joe Wheeler, who became my new dad. I knew he was going to be really neat because, for my ninth birthday, he gave me a real J. C. Higgins BB gun! My new dad came with a great new uncle named Jack Wheeler. Jack lived in the mountains of Lockwood Valley, California, which is about a ninety-minute drive north of Los Angeles. To a frustrated Davy Crockett "wanna be" city dweller like me, Lockwood Valley was heaven on earth. After all, what more could a boy who had been bitten by the "Crockett bug" want but real mountains and a real BB gun?!

Shortly after my mom and Joe Wheeler married, we moved into my great uncle's cabin in Lockwood Valley and my dream of being a mountain man became a reality. I was elated to visit him. As far as I was concerned, Uncle Jack lived in the middle of a paradise where I could take my BB gun and hunt deer, mountain lions, rabbits, quail, and rattlesnakes! My mind reasoned that I could live off the land. The nearest town was Frasier Park, and it was twenty miles away.

I liked spending time with my new dad. He seemed so big and strong, standing a handsome six feet, two inches tall. He would often take me to town with him. One day, while we were driving to Frasier Park for supplies, I began to realize that I had a problem. I recall my new dad trying to teach me to spell my new last name –*W-h-e-e-l-e-r*. Then and there, at the age of nine, I discovered that I could *not* even spell my birth name, Richard Basil Lobato. I couldn't spell, read, or write simple words. I suddenly knew why my report cards referred to me as being "retarded."

The Lord used Joe Wheeler as the first special instrument to cause me to begin the disciplines of learning to think, concentrate, memorize, and develop effective study habits. I could speak fluent Spanish and English, but my book learning was way behind. Until the age of twelve, I couldn't read and could barely write my own name. However, God was gracious to give me Joe Wheeler for a dad. He and Mr. Wells, who was my sixth-grade teacher, took special time to help me. With their encouragement and my hard work trying to focus and sit still long enough to concentrate, I was finally able to read by the time I entered seventh grade. Amazingly, in one year, I could read through complete books and had developed successful study skills. I even learned most of my multiplication tables that year. My newfound ability to read opened a whole new world for me to explore. I began to read all I could find on cowboys, gunfighters, Indians, mountain men, and soldiers of the Old West.

Most people can look back over their lives and remember the "golden years." For me, the "golden years" in Lockwood Valley were too short-lived. I remember going out for long walks in the mountains just to explore. I loved to walk and talk with God and spend time discovering His marvelous creation. The cabin was primitive since Uncle Jack had built it himself many years before he moved into it, which was shortly after World War I. He homesteaded the 160 acres upon which the cabin was located. A wood stove was the only source of heat, so I was given the task of chopping wood for it. We even used an old-fashioned outhouse that had real bullet holes in it, which made me often wonder if I was going to get shot while using it.

One summer, while exploring, I escaped from a life-threatening experience. I was only nine years old and a complete novice to outdoor life, which made me unaware of certain dangers. I recall hearing a buzzing sound unlike anything I had ever heard before. I slowly began to walk around in the nearby trees assuming that the buzzing was a humming bird. As I walked backwards, the sound became very pronounced and, as I turned around, I could see, to my complete shock and surprise, that I had cornered a huge rattlesnake! The coiled snake was on the edge of a bluff and was ready to strike if I were to take another step toward it. I am sure, since I was so young and inexperienced, that had I been bitten, I would have run with all my might back to the cabin, which was about two miles away, causing the poison to travel very quickly to my heart. In that case, I am convinced that I would have died before reaching the cabin. However, the Lord had further use for me and spared me from being bitten by the snake.

I was in such a panic that I *did* run all the way back to the cabin. In fact, I ran so fast that a hound dog couldn't have caught me. As I ran, all I could think of was, "This is crazy! Why am I running so fast and out of control? I might run into another snake!"

In spite of the logic, I couldn't keep myself from running as fast as my legs would carry me so I could be back home safe. Like myself, many children often think they are "grown up" and like to wander away from home, but whenever the snakes of life coil up to strike us, we always go running back home where it is safely and warmly protected by our parents. It is sad to think that many children don't have stable families to run home to for protection.

The summers were so hot that a person could have cooked eggs on a rock. The winters were so cold in the rock-hewn cabin with no insulation, that I can distinctly recall waking up in the middle of the night with my nose and ears ice cold. I would have to put my head under the blankets to keep from freezing to death only to begin to suffocate and then have to take them off again to breathe. This process of breathing ice-cold air and then covering up with blankets would go on all night long. When I got up in the morning, the cabin would be so cold that any water that was left standing in the sinks had frozen solid. Once the potbelly wood stove was lit, I would stand close by to warm my front side while my backside froze. I would keep turning myself rotisserie style to keep warm all over.

Going to school was a major ordeal. Our home was the farthest from the school. So, we had to walk that proverbial mile to the bus stop so we could be the first to be picked up at 7:00 a.m. Oftentimes, after a snowstorm, this meant trudging through three feet of snow, which is really deep when you are only four feet tall! This also meant that, after school, we were the last to arrive home, which was around 4:30 p.m. Despite seemingly bleak and miserable conditions, I loved every moment and would not want to trade one of those days for all the luxuries and mansions that rich and privileged children enjoy while growing up. Very few children can say that during the winter they had to sit on their hands in an outhouse to keep from being stuck frozen to the seat! Yes sir, I was on the way to becoming a future Davy Crockett!

CHAPTER 5

Sad Days Ahead

My dream of being Davy Crockett, mountain man and trapper was abruptly broken when the day came that my dad told Sylvia and me that we were going to have to move back to Los Angeles. Being young and, like most children, resilient, I made the best of the situation. Besides, I figured we could always come back on weekends and during summer months. At the time, I didn't fully realize that mom and dad were not getting along.

Shortly after moving to Culver City, California, mom and dad began to fight frequently. I remember times when I was lying in bed during the middle of the night that their arguments ended up in fist-fighting. Many times, I wondered if they would kill each other. Sometimes the fights were so violent that mother would grab a kitchen knife to defend herself. Scared and alone in my room, I would pray that the Lord Jesus would come and sit on my bed to comfort and protect me. I would ask God to make Mom and Dad stop fighting. I always felt the comfort and presence of the Lord during those difficult times. As a young child, I didn't know the words of Psalm 91:1-2, *"He that dwelleth in the secret place of the most High shall abide under the shadow of the Almighty. I will say of the LORD, He is my refuge and my fortress: my God; in him will I trust."* However, I did experience the truth of these verses within my spirit and I learned later as a Christian man to know and love them.

I still longed to escape back into the wilderness to live a simple way of life. In part, my desire became a reality when my mother legally separated from dad and moved us to Santa Monica, California, where we lived only five blocks from the beach. I loved my Santa Monica years. Where there is a will, there is a way. I soon found a way to fulfill my dream of being a trapper despite living in the city. I set up a trapping line for gophers in my neighborhood. I skinned and cured each pelt of the small pocket gophers that I trapped. I was so very proud of those choice prizes. I had several pelts on my dresser to lay my wallet, comb, and change on. I even had a pelt mounted on my wall just like a real mountain man would have put on his cabin wall. I had finally become a trapper. Mother didn't know quite what to do with her "retarded gopher trapper." Whenever I showed her my prized pelts, she would just smile and humor me by saying, "That's nice." Along with trapping, I picked up a knife and found that it substituted quite well for a tomahawk. So, I spent hours throwing knives at the big old magnolia trees in our front yard.

I didn't have the type of personality that gravitated toward a multitude of friends, but I did select a few close ones near my home. Across the street lived a Catholic boy just slightly younger than I, named Randy Como. Randy also came from a broken home, so we related well to each other and soon developed a close friendship. Around the corner lived Billy Davis, who became a lifelong friend. Up the street lived Mark Pellet. By the time I entered seventh grade, all four of us were very close and, at times, inseparable.

It seemed that even from my early years on, although I was not scholastically gifted, I had leadership qualities. The Lord used me to influence my friends to be interested in the outdoors, hunting, by going to my Uncle Jack's cabin whenever possible. Since we lived so close to the beach, we also took up surfing during the Beach Boys' heyday and their hit song, "Surfing U.S.A." As far back as I can recall, I was always a leader not a follower. Friends did what I chose to do, not what they wanted. This kept me out of a lot of trouble, because I generally chose things that were right for the fear I had of displeasing the Lord.

Children are born into this world despite the difficulties of a marriage. During those sad and turbulent times, my parents did try to make their marriage succeed. As a result, my two half sisters, Elizabeth and Anna, were born. I was a very attentive older brother. I also loved having younger sisters who didn't think I was "retarded" and over whom I could be boss. Older brothers are always very smart in the eyes of their younger siblings. In many ways, my younger sisters helped build my confidence and contributed to my learning how to be a future father. My older sister, Sylvia, and I were not very compatible growing up. Living in a dysfunctional home often does not provide an environment that encourages love and respect between siblings.

CHAPTER 6

Training in Stewardship

My first and most amazing job was when I was just a little guy of eight years old in the 1950s. I was hired by the *Los Angeles Times* to sell newspapers in the middle of the street on the islands where people boarded the electric streetcars, now obsolete. I had one of those money change gizmos around my waist, so that I could give change to drivers when they rolled down their windows to buy a paper before the light turned green. It was hopping work during rush hour.

Today, companies cannot legally hire under-aged children to do the work I loved to do back then. In those days, if I didn't work, I couldn't buy what I needed, which included necessary things like shoes and clothing. We were a poor family, and my mother worked out of necessity, especially since my dad would come and go depending on how the marriage was going. Out of that same necessity, I had to learn to save money at an early age. Coming from a poor family caused me to work for things I wanted or needed.

Purchasing items taught me many valuable lessons early in life. For example, I recall when transistor radios were just coming into vogue and I wanted one very badly. So, I saved the necessary fourteen dollars to purchase a radio, which in those days was a considerable fortune for a young lad. My mother took me shopping for my prized radio. I spotted one in a store window and bought it on sight. It was a two-transistor pocket model. I was as happy as a lark until, about two blocks away, I saw a more powerful six-transistor radio for the same amount of money! Oh, I was sure disturbed that I didn't take the time to shop around and compare prices! To this day, I haven't forgotten that experience or the lesson it taught me. As a result, it has saved me thousands of dollars over the years.

By the time I was fifteen years old, my mother allowed me to buy my first firearms with the money I had earned through my industrious work. I bought a .22 caliber Winchester; a Savage over and under 22/20 gauge shotgun combination, and a Colt 38 single-action revolver. The revolver was my pride and joy because it was a *real* Old West gunfighter's gun. By doing odd jobs throughout my junior high years, I was able to amass quite an arsenal for such a young lad.

The Lord has always gifted me with the ability to secure work and save money, which has enabled me to purchase items with cash. I have always enjoyed work, and I am fond of many of the Proverbs in the Bible that deal with the rewards of working hard such as Proverbs 10:4, *"He becometh poor that dealeth with a slack hand, but the hand of the diligent maketh rich."*

I learned another life changing lesson regarding money when I was about seventeen years old. For some crazy reason, a local Santa Monica department store called Campbell's allowed me to secure an in-store charge card. It was my first charge card, and I felt very big and grandiose to be able to buy things just like adults. It happened to be during the Christmas season, and I decided to charge all my Christmas gifts in that one store. Every member of my family was impressed by the selection of gifts I had purchased for them. You can imagine the shock

21

I received when I got my first bill at the beginning of the New Year! I began to make my monthly payments and couldn't help but notice how long it took for me to pay off the bill. It felt as if I were on a long hike going up a very steep hill and that I would never reach the summit. I finally did reach the summit by the following November—just a month before the next Christmas! By that time, I had paid twice the original amount charged because of the accumulated interest. Even though I was a bit dim witted, I learned that charging on credit was an expensive proposition. When Christmas came again, I decided not to charge anything that I couldn't payoff in cash by the time the bill was due the following month. Christmas was lean for all my family members that year, but I was much richer and felt much freer. For over thirty years now, I have made it a policy to live as the old Amish proverb says, "Spend less than you earn, and you will never be in debt."

CHAPTER 7

Joyful Years

Back in the early 1960s, it was relatively safe to allow children to go to the park to play hide-and-seek until 10:00 p.m. Generally, children could just hang around the neighborhood without fear of being kidnapped or any of the other dangers that plague our present lawless society, which is devoid of God's moral laws.

My mother used to allow me the joy and freedom of boarding the Santa Monica Greyhound bus to travel the 100 miles to Lockwood Valley. Packing my .22 caliber Winchester and rifle bag, I was off for a glorious weekend. Oftentimes, my uncle would pick me up from the bus station. Other times, I would just hitchhike a ride to the cabin. Sadly, those relatively safe days are now gone.

Once I arrived at the cabin, I would begin hunting jackrabbits. One might say I graduated from small game, pocket gophers, to big game, jackrabbits. I stalked those prized varmints just as I imagined my heroes Davy Crockett, Kit Carson, Joe Meek, and Jed Smith would do. After shooting them in the head, as Annie Oakley would have done, I skinned 'em, cooked 'em, on the old wood stove, and ate 'em. On my weekend cabin adventures, I lived off what I hunted and, I have to admit, I always looked forward to returning home on Sunday afternoons to Mom's homemade Mexican food, which was the best in the Southwest.

My cabin adventures were very rewarding. I gained a sense of well being while learning to be a provider, and I had the opportunity to spend time with Uncle Jack who *never* put me down by calling me "retarded." Oftentimes, I would go out alone and just walk and talk with Jesus while enjoying the smell of sage brush and pine trees. While I enjoyed returning to Mom's cooking on Sunday afternoons, I dreaded going back to school on Monday mornings. I attended John Adams Junior High School, which was located in a rough section of Santa Monica. There was always tension between the blacks, the Mexicans, and the surfers. Daily, I had to fight my way through school to keep my lunch and my reputation. Today, I can't begin to imagine sending my own children to the same types of schools that I attended. My educational experience was not all that desirable even though I attended school back during the good old "happy days" of the 1950s and 1960s. In most subjects, I barely passed. My grades were mostly Cs and Ds. However, I did show some promise in subjects such as history, music, and theater carrying B averages. It is interesting to note that all of the classes that I performed well in are now of use in my life's vocation. *"The steps of a good man are ordered by the Lord: and he delighteth in his way"* (Psalm 37:23).

CHAPTER 8

The Kiss of Death

Besides identifying with Davy Crockett as portrayed by Fess Parker, I had another role model. Since I enjoyed singing, I looked up to pop singer Andy Williams. I used to sing along with many of his records, and my goal was to be a performer like him someday. The kids at school thought I was "touched in the head" because I liked Andy so much. This was especially so, because, in those days, demonic rock music began to emerge out of the pit of hell and groups like the Rolling Stones, Black Sabbath, and Grateful Dead were making inroads into the youth scene. My admiration of Andy Williams was definitely NOT "cool." I stayed clear of those groups along with the promiscuous living and the drugs that came with the rock culture. Thus, it was Andy Williams who had a much more profound influence on me. *"He that walketh with wise men shall be wise; but a companion of fools shall be destroyed"* (Proverbs 13:20).

Foolish and promiscuous women who lack virtue and morals destroyed both Samson and Solomon. Sadly, many a young and strong moral man has also succumbed to the enchantments and charms of a beautiful wayward woman. These men, who lack understanding, become ensnared by the deceitful look of a woman, which is exactly what so many of the Proverbs warn young men against. When I was in the eleventh grade, the demons of lust went on the warpath against me. I was very shy and naturally reserved around females. I grew up in schools that separated the boys from the girls. During class time, the girls sat with the girls, and the boys sat with the boys. In grammar school, we had a girl's line and a boy's line, and we were not allowed to talk to each other except on a passing basis.

One day, while in my junior year, a girl named Louisa Pepronni came up to me and asked me for a date. She was like an Italian pizza—full of the spice of life. Her asking me out made me nervous, yet I was flattered, so I consented. Since I had never been on a date and had no idea what to do, I sought advice by telling the guys during P.E. class that Louisa and I were planning to go out. They made baboon sounds and said, "All right, dude! Cool!"

I didn't know what it all meant at the time, but I soon found out. "What does a person do on a date?" I asked.

They told me to "take her to dinner, and after that would come the fun part."

They further instructed me to "proceed to the beach parking lot and kiss her."

I was shocked! "Kiss?" I asked. "Do you mean like I kiss my mom and sisters before I go to bed?"

"Nooo, n-e-r-d Wheeler! We'll tell you how to kiss her."

And they did. I was completely grossed out.

"I can't do that!" I exclaimed. "I'll get mononucleosis!"

"No you won't," they said. "You get 'mono' by sharing R. C. Colas."

I don't remember where we went to dinner that night. I was too nervous to recall such details. I do remember that I took my 1956 four-door Ford station wagon down to the beach to do what my friends expected me to do. I was so naive that I left the back seat folded down where I kept a mattress to sleep on for when I went camping and surfing along the Southern California beaches. Innocently, I did not realize what the implications were or how it looked to others.

When Louisa saw where we were heading, she jumped over the front seat of the car into the back seat and lay down on the mattress and said, "I'm waiting for you."

I was so scared that I proceeded to drive all around the parking lot until Louisa finally demanded, "What's taking so long?"

"I'm looking for the right spot," I told her.

I finally found the "right spot" when I stopped in front of her house. I stepped out of the driver's seat, opened the back door of my station wagon, and asked her to get out. I sent her into her house that night without so much as a good night kiss. I was afraid that if I kissed Louisa my destiny would be to burn in hell eternally. Naturally, my fear was founded on good reason. Years later, after I was born again, I discovered that *"whoremongers . . . shall have their part in the lake which burneth with fire and brimstone"* (Revelation 21:8).

I am fully convinced that we, as parents, must teach the "fear of the Lord" to our children, which is much neglected in this present day. The devil has used the lust of the flesh to destroy many people over the generations. My early Roman Catholic training in the "fear of the Lord" proved me in good stead to help me keep on the "straight and narrow." John Wycliffe (c.1334-1384) once wrote:

Also, most of all fear God and His wrath; and love God and His law, and His worship; and ask not principally for worldly reward, but in all thine heart desire the bliss of heaven, and the mercy of God, and a holy life; and think often on the dreadful doom of the pains of hell, in order to keep thee out of sin; and on the endless great joys of life; and according to thy skill teach others to do the same.

CHAPTER 9

The Zeal of the Lord

From 1966 until 1972, when I was between eighteen and twenty-three years of age, I was lost and confused amidst my religious activities, trying to find a profession and "myself." Religiously, I became more zealous in trying to please God, but I was always frustrated. Somehow, I felt that I just couldn't do enough to serve the Lord and make Him happy so that He would accept me. The more I tried to please the Lord, the more I still felt that I was not good enough for Him. There were times when I would sleep on the floor, next to my bed, to signify to the Lord that I wanted to mortify the flesh and draw closer to Him. At times, in penance, I would take a belt and lash my back. It was never enough.

I joined an organization in my local parish called the Legion of Mary. In the Legion, I was committed to pray the rosary three times a day (fifty-nine prayers on each rosary) for a total of 177 prayers a day, seven days a week. At the Legion's midweek evening service, I was always punctual to pray the rosary with others. On Saturdays, I would go door-to-door to share my Roman Catholic faith, and I made myself available to pray for the sick, to encourage families to pray and go to church—ultimately, to hunger for the Lord. I would hand out picture prayer cards to families visiting our services. The card had a prayer on the back and a saint's picture on the front so that the person could invoke the saint needed to meet his or her prayer needs.

I knew that I still wasn't doing enough to please God, so I began attending a Mormon Church with a girl from my high school. We were both in the Santa Monica High choral singing group, the Madrigals. I read the *Book of Mormon, Pearl of Great Price,* and *Doctrines and Covenants.* My Mormon escapade didn't last long, because I always feared that going to a non-Catholic church was a sin. During my school days of religious Catholic training, this teaching was drilled into my head.

Not long after leaving the Mormon Church, I felt led to inquire of God again,—outside the Roman Catholic Church. I began to pursue instruction with the Jehovah's Witnesses, but I continued to feel empty inside as I knew that God was still not completely pleased with me.

There seemed to be no end to the despair that I felt in trying to gain God's favor. After work, I used to drive to a local Roman Catholic church, where I would spend thirty minutes in prayer kneeling before lighted candles and various statues asking them to pray for me so that I could gain God's love and attention. In the mornings, I would go to church at six o'clock for early mass and serve as an altar boy for the priest.

I thank God that during those days, the Lord continued to have His hand upon my life. I didn't fully understand it at the time, but I always felt that He did love me and would guide me. I loved Him dearly, and the thoughts of the Lord were always on my mind. I longed and desired to have and feel a personal relationship with Him. I wouldn't give up my search until I had the security of *knowing* His love for me. My dilemma was *how* to obtain my desire. I began to grow weary in my search for God because I was spending so much time and effort at working hard in my flesh to please Him. At the time, I didn't know that it was by *His Spirit* and not by my might that I would find Him. I thank God that, by His love and grace, He saw my heart's desire and found me. *"One thing have I desired of the LORD, that will I seek after; that I may dwell in the house of the LORD all the days of my life, to behold the beauty of the LORD, and to inquire in his temple"* (Psalm 27:4).

"I sought the LORD, and He heard me, and delivered me from all my fears" (Psalm 34:4).

The Bible promises that those who hope in the Lord *will* be satisfied. I did have hope, and the LORD must have seen my heart's desire for Him. *"Blessed is the man that trusteth in the LORD, and whose hope the Lord is. For he shall be as a tree planted by the waters, and that spreadeth out her roots by the river, and shall not see when heat cometh, but her leaf shall be green; and shall not be careful in the year of drought, neither shall cease from yielding fruit. The heart is deceitful above all things, and desperately wicked: who can know it? I the LORD search the heart, I try the reins, even to give every man according to his ways, and according to the fruit of his doings"* *(Jeremiah 17:7-10).*

In an unusual way, the Lord began to answer my prayers when I was only seventeen years old. I was working as a bus boy after school at Manning's Cafeteria in Santa Monica. We had regular customers who always came in to eat their evening meals. There was an older couple whom I had grown very fond of, although I don't remember their names today. However, I do remember that their manners and expressions were unusual. They had a peaceful countenance and were always kind and gentle of spirit.

One day, they left me a dollar tip along with a black, Gideon New Testament and Psalms pocket Bible. It was the first Bible that I had ever owned and the greatest tip that I had ever received! In retrospect, I now realize that those sweet people were Christians. Their faces were radiant with the love of God. For all the hundreds of faces I had known by the age of seventeen, in my mind's eye, they stood apart from all the rest. They gave me *the* Bible that the Lord used to shape and direct my steps. In fact, it was the same Bible that illuminated my path and led me to my Savior, Jesus Christ.

I read that particular Bible all the time. I sat and cried while reading the teachings of Christ. I rejoiced when I read the parts where Jesus healed and forgave sinners. I treasured that Bible and its teachings which I supernaturally received by reading it. Those teachings were to be of the utmost value to me in the years to come.

CHAPTER 10

The Steps of a Righteous Man

Throughout my high school years, I continued going to Lockwood Valley as often as possible so that I could practice my quick draw, shooting, throwing my knife and tomahawk. I skinned varmints and roped neighbors while they were mowing the grass. While in school, I found joy in taking a drama class and singing with the prestigious Madrigals. I thoroughly enjoyed performing on stage. Stage fright was foreign to me as I have never experienced it whatsoever.

My dad, Joe Wheeler, encouraged me to study mechanical drafting. I didn't like drafting, but I did it out of respect for my dad. When I graduated from high school mid-term, in 1967, I immediately entered Los Angeles Trade Tech to continue my mechanical drafting studies.

The following spring, I entered a talent contest. I selected a song that Andy Williams had made popular at the time. The song was taken from his hit album, *Call Me Irresponsible*. After my performance, the pianist took me aside to tell me that I had great potential to be a performer and that I should seek to develop my talent. That was all I needed to hear to set me afire. I finished my term at the trade school and transferred to Santa Monica College where I could study to earn a major in music/theater and a minor in history. Reluctantly, my dad agreed. I felt, that without a doubt, the Lord was leading me down the right path. I also began private voice training and secured some amateur acting parts and opportunities to sing in various places throughout Southern California.

For America, those were difficult days as the Vietnam Conflict was in full swing. I was of the age that I could have been drafted at any time. My friend, Billy Davis, was drafted and sent to Southeast Asia. When I said farewell to Billy, I wondered if I would ever see him again.

At that time, how could I know that Billy Davis and I would have a special link in the years to come? As I would eventually learn, the Lord unfolds His seemingly mysterious will for the lives of His chosen people who are called in Christ Jesus.

CHAPTER 11

Friends are from God

While I pursued the performing arts and was trained by various singing instructors over a period of two years, the Lord directed my steps to one very special singing coach. God used him in a profound way to help prepare, mold, and shape my life for public ministry. At the time, I still wasn't saved and was unaware of the Biblical principle, *"For my thoughts are not your thoughts, neither are your ways my ways, saith the LORD"* (Isaiah 55:8).

At that time, the Lord had plans for me that I could not even begin to imagine. *"Eye hath not seen, nor ear heard, neither have entered into the heart of man, the things which God hath prepared for them that love him"* (I Corinthians 2:9).

My new vocal instructor's name was Earl Brent. Earl lived in Brentwood, California, and he gave singing instruction in his home. When we first met, he introduced me to his sweet mother who was living with him. Earl was a bachelor in his mid-fifties, and his mother was in her seventies.

For my first lesson, Earl began by giving me a voice check. Within a few minutes, he discerned that I had potential. Unfortunately, he also noticed the damage other so-called voice instructors had done to my voice. He spent over a year retraining and correcting my voice. In a humble manner, he took time and spent several hours with me sharing his musical career and accomplishments. To say the least, I was impressed. Earl had worked as a pianist, for over thirteen years, at MGM in Culver City during its

"Golden Years." He knew all the great actors such as Clark Gable, Lana Turner, Spencer Tracy, Henry Fonda, and James Stewart. Earl had learned many tricks-of-the-trade from those great stars, and he passed their performing secrets on to me.

Earl Brent also knew every major musical performer, composer, and musician of that time. He was Judy Garland's personal pianist during her tours. Earl had helped write a multitude of songs for MGM studios. He teamed with great songwriters of the day who wrote the famous musicals of the 1940s and 1950s. During the years that Earl instructed me, he earned his income writing nightclub acts for performers. The best known were Frank Sinatra and Jack Jones.

Being young and somewhat naive I took the opportunity of asking Earl what the real show biz world was like, especially, behind the scenes away from the public eye. I wanted to know what the performers and actors were really like when they were not performing. Earl's answers kept me from becoming star-struck and from seeking fame and glory. I perceived the shallowness of the Hollywood crowd, yet, strangely, I continued training with him. In fact, I was amazed that he would even want to consider continuing to work with me. At first, we had weekly lessons that lasted an hour and a half at a time. The expense was great, but to me the lessons were invaluable. Much of what I am today, I owe, in thanks, to the Lord for sending me to Earl Brent. Earl was, for me, as Elijah was for Elisha. Earl had never married nor had children, so he practically adopted me. Over the years we became best of friends, much like David and Jonathan of the Bible.

As our friendship grew, Earl began to meet with me several times a week. Not only did he train me to sing, but he also trained me to project my timid speaking voice, to walk into a room with a stage presence, to greet people, and to be well-mannered. Growing up in a dysfunctional family, I lacked many skills. Earl and I traveled throughout Southern California performing in various settings, I singing and he as my accompanying pianist.

Eventually, Earl met my future wife, Marilyn, and was my best man at our wedding. He lived long enough to see and meet our first daughter, Noelle. I was at Earl's side when his beloved mother passed away and was used by the Lord to help comfort him through those rough days. We would spend hours talking about Christ and His Kingdom. Earl told me that, when he died, he wanted me to be the beneficiary of his estate and to receive the royalties to the songs he had written over the years. Being young, I was not too sure what he was talking about, so I always graciously changed the subject. I wanted him to know that I loved him, not for what he would leave to me when he died, but for his friendship to me while he lived.

When Earl died of cancer in 1977, I lost an irreplaceable and dearly beloved friend. Death is an enemy that is despised, but thanks be to God, as Christians, we have the hope that we will be reunited with our loved ones who have gone on before us to our Lord and Savior Jesus Christ. Jesus said, *"I am the resurrection, and the life: he that believeth in me, though he were dead, yet shall he live: And whosoever liveth and believeth in me shall never die..."* (John 11:25-26). My prayer is that Earl Brent and I will live on the same block in the "City of Gold" throughout eternity. The inheritance he left me was an immeasurable gift that the Lord used to launch me into full-time ministry.

CHAPTER 12

Girl of My Dreams

I have grown to appreciate Proverbs 19:14, *"House and riches are the inheritance of fathers: and a prudent wife is from the LORD,"* and Proverbs 18:22, *"Whoso findeth a wife findeth a good thing, and obtaineth favor of the LORD."* The longer I am married, the more I am convinced that a man without a God-fearing woman influencing his life can be dangerous to himself and to the society in which he lives. As I look back over the years, I am truly grateful for my virtuous wife, Marilyn. Between her stabilizing influence in my life and my own discernment, we have been able to avoid many disasters that potentially can plague a modern person's life.

Let me jump back to 1968 before Earl passed away and when I was working as a stock boy for Leroy's Jewelers in the outdoor street mall in Santa Monica. The Christmas season was in full swing, and Leroy's hired three part-time girls from Santa Monica High School to help with gift-wrapping. I became acquainted with each of the girls and treated them with respect and was careful to maintain a friendly business relationship. Throughout the month of November, I was able to observe and judge the character of each girl. One of them, Marilyn Cobb, was especially polite, kind, attentive, responsible, diligent, witty, and smart. It didn't take long for her to capture my full attention.

I decided to ask Marilyn for a date, which was highly unusual for me, since I was very reserved and shy around girls. It took a considerable amount of courage for me just to ask her out. My heart was pounding so hard that I was sure she could see my shirt rising and lowering with each heartbeat. Marilyn was flattered and accepted my invitation. However, she was a bit apprehensive, and reasonably so, because she was only sixteen years old and I was almost twenty. As a precautionary measure, she wisely arranged for us to double date. We went to Santa Monica College, where I was still a student, to see a theater play. Since I was in the theater arts department at the time, I pointed out the various performers on stage and related bits of information that I had gathered while working with the performers in previous productions.

When the play was over, we separated from our double dating partners, and I walked Marilyn to her apartment door to say thank you and good night. In those godless days of the "free love" revolution, it was customary, as it is today, to kiss your date good night. However, I liked Marilyn so much, and had such a respect for her, that I decided not to risk our potential relationship by giving her a kiss. Besides, she was so nervous that she broke out all over her neck with big red blotches. I thought she had some kind of disease! I walked away hoping that she would consider going out with me again.

The following day was my twentieth birthday, and I had a contract to sing at a USO facility in Hollywood, so I called Marilyn and invited her to go with me. She declined, saying she had a bad cold and had to do her homework.

"How do you like that?" I said to myself. "She turned me down for *homework*! She certainly can't be too interested in me."

On Monday, after school, Marilyn returned to work. I was hesitant to face her again, but she came up to me and gave me a birthday card. Lo and behold, she did care for me! That card got me a wife, as I knew, right then and there, that she was the one for me! After our second date, I told Marilyn that I was going to marry her someday. The Lord had given me a peace in my heart that He had brought Marilyn into my life. She was the girl of my dreams. However, from the very start, our relationship presented many seemingly impossible obstacles.

Marilyn was not only the most beautiful girl in the world but she also possessed the brains I never had. The problem became obvious when I began to share with her the most *important* things to me and my life—hunting, skinning varmints, camping, hiking, the outdoors, guns, knives, and all the craziness of the Crockett instinct in me. While I collected guns in high school, Marilyn, being an advocate of gun control, sat at the Santa Monica Mall, in front of J. C. Penney's, to get citizens to register for gun control in defiance of gun lovers—like me!

Talk about opposites!

I liked going to Uncle Jack's cabin, but she would freak out because she didn't like seeing all the dead animals hanging on the wall. Marilyn had never even left the Santa Monica area in her entire life, mostly, because her father was too busy working. Her father was a stereotypical frugal Scotsman who seldom spent time or money to give his family what he called "wasteful" indulgences such as vacations, restaurants, and Disneyland.

I liked horseback riding, while Marilyn hardly enjoyed bike riding. Yes, indeed, Marilyn had all the characteristics of being a traitor to everything I held dear to my heart. However, despite our differences, I loved her. Little did I know, the Lord was using her to tame my barbarian nature. Had I known, I would have fled in terror!

One beautiful spring day, I decided to take Marilyn out of town for a drive up to the Los Angeles Mountains. It was one of those rare and wonderful smog-free days that offers a beautiful view from San Bernardino all the way to the Pacific Ocean. After our picnic, we headed home. While winding down the mountain on a two-lane road, I suddenly stopped on the roadside and exclaimed, "Did you see that?"

She was certain that something was terribly wrong. I explained to her that I had just seen a bushy gray squirrel that had been hit by a car but whose pelt was still in good condition. I further informed her that I was fixing to skin the varmint.

I told her, "This is a rare find! All my life, I've wanted a pelt like this one, but, usually, I only find pelts that have been mangled by tires leaving the body so squished that I can't do anything but cut off the tail to hang on my rear-view mirror."

Excited, I continued to explain the procedure to Marilyn. Her face became alarmingly contorted. I couldn't imagine why. After I finished my discourse on skinning road kill, she let out a high-pitched shriek and then yelled, "If you touch that dead animal and attempt to bring it into this car, I am going to walk home!"

Now, I had known her for several months, but I had never seen her so upset. What was I to do? The moment had arrived! I had to *choose* between Marilyn and that longed-for squirrel pelt which was a rare find. What a choice! After what seemed like an eternity, I reluctantly pulled the car onto the road and headed back toward civilization. The tug-of-war had begun. It was a pull that was going to begin to establish priorities in my previously uncivilized life. Within two years, I had become so civilized that I had sold all my guns and gotten rid of all my gopher, rabbit, and snake skins. My alias school name, *The Cherokee Kid,* was replaced with just plain old *Richard Wheeler.*

That wasn't the only change the Lord was making. He continued to use Marilyn to set a course for me that would make me a useful instrument for His Kingdom. As a good Catholic boy, I was expected to get married and raise my children within the Roman Catholic Church. Herein was another one of our differences and a problem—to say the least. Marilyn had been raised by an atheistic father who was hostile toward the Gospel of Christ. Surprisingly, Marilyn was not as hostile and was more of an agnostic than an atheist in her beliefs. She wanted proof and needed convincing that there was a God with whom she could have a personal relationship. When I suggested to her that we attend new convert classes, she willingly consented. I bought her a Catholic Bible, and she began to read it and attend religious studies once a week. It didn't take very long for her intellect to find inconsistencies between the Catholic Bible and the doctrine we were receiving on Wednesday nights at convert class. Being so steeped in the Catholic faith, I had never seen what she saw so clearly.

When she pointed out the inconsistencies, we asked Father McCarthy to explain why he was teaching slightly different views from that of the Catholic Bible. He attempted to answer our questions to the best of his ability, and we were somewhat satisfied. However, as the class progressed we became a bone of contention to poor Father McCarthy as we challenged him week after week. Finally, in exasperation, he told us not to ask questions any more. He further explained that the Roman Catholic Church was God's *divine* church and that it was infallible in all areas. It was a *must* that we simply trust the Church but it was too late–I was changing. No longer was I satisfied with glib answers to my important questions. Deep down inside, I felt that I was being deceived. I began to pray, asking Jesus Himself to show me the truth.

CHAPTER 13

Searching for the Truth

Not too long after Father McCarthy had mandated that our questioning cease, Marilyn and I were walking along the Santa Monica beach promenade. During our quiet moments, I meditated on which church was the *true one*. By this time, I had already dabbled in Mormonism and the Jehovah's Witnesses. I was truly seeking direction from the true and living God.

As we walked along the beachfront, a total stranger walked up to us and asked, "Do you want to know the truth?"

I was shocked. This was the very prayer that I had been praying! "Yes!" I exclaimed. "I've been searching for the truth for a long time and to no avail."

The man told me, "My name is Joseph, and I attend a church that meets in a home in Los Angeles." Then he gave us the address.

Marilyn and I eagerly showed up for our first Bible study. I was so excited to find the *"deeper truth"* that I swallowed the whole pill and quickly joined the Unification Church. I had become a Moonie.

Marilyn was not as easily convinced. Being naturally skeptical, she kept reserved and at a distance. She continued her search and attended the meetings with caution. I, on the other hand, was so hungry for God that I couldn't get enough with just a once-a-week teaching. My lifetime desire had caused me to face the most difficult decision of my life. The burning question was, "Would I leave my family and my promised someday-to-be wife to move in with the Moonies, so that I could further pursue the revelations of Reverend Sun Yung Moon?"

The hardest part was saying good-bye to Marilyn. I remember, vividly, walking her around the block to tell her where I was going and that I wouldn't be able to call her or see her nearly as often because the Moonies would be controlling my "comings and goings." Also, I explained to her that I would have to bring a Moonie with me whenever I did visit with her, so that I wouldn't be influenced to fall away from what they called "The Divine Principle." Marilyn was compliant, in her usual sweet way, but I could tell she was hurt.

As we continued our walk, the struggle within me became so great that I had an emotional breakdown. I fell down on the grass, beside the sidewalk, and started groaning and wailing. I was crying so loudly that the neighbors thought someone was killing me. I couldn't control my sobbing. Staggering to my feet, I hobbled to my car before the neighbors had a chance to call the police. I was so torn apart emotionally that I cried during the entire drive to Los Angeles. All I could think about was, "How could I choose between my deep love for Marilyn and my loving desire for God?"

I would not, for all the wealth of the world, go through that terrible experience again. God and Satan were waging battle and contending for my soul. I was being "rent in twain."

Ultimately, I couldn't deny God, so I decided to move in with the Unification Church. Immediately, I began turning over my paycheck to them for room and board. Every evening, after work, we received indoctrination. I felt somewhat consoled by the fact that God couldn't help but be more pleased with my ascetic life-style. Surely, He would notice my fasting and late night studies with my new "family" members.

Yet, even with all my increased religious activities, I still felt empty inside. I couldn't escape the feeling that I was still not pleasing God enough to gain His favor. I continued to take voice lessons and visit with my family and Marilyn by sneaking out. Moonies were very adamant about keeping their new converts away from the influence of anyone who was, as they termed, "unsaved." They feared that we would turn away from the Unification Church and return to our former life.

One night, I decided to sneak out and share the teachings of the Unification Church. I drove to Griffith Park Observatory, which is in the foothills of Los Angeles and not too far away from where I had lived. I saw a man standing, all alone, right outside the main entrance of the observatory. He looked like the typical hippie of the 1970s with a long, straggly beard and that kind of "spaced-out" look. I decided that he would be the one to whom I would witness and share the teachings of the Unification Church.

I spent about twenty minutes sharing "The Divine Principles" of Reverend Sun Yung Moon with him and what I thought to be the reality of life. The man responded to me by slapping the side of a huge granite stone fence that surrounded the observatory saying, "Nothing is *real*! This building is not *real*. 'The Divine Principle' is not *real*!"

I thought, "Wow! This is really profound. I have met a man who knows some *other* TRUTH!" I was very excited to hear that neither the Moonies nor their teachings were *real*. Finally, I had the reason I needed to leave the group. If I could just find someone who could disprove them, then I could leave with a clear conscience that I hadn't offended God and I could go back home to Marilyn.

I asked the man who had this other "truth" to come home with me so he could tell everyone of this profound reality—that nothing was real and it was all just an illusion. The man refused my request. He told me that I had to find this "truth" for myself and that I would have to tell it to everyone myself. With great excitement, I hurried back to the Moonies to tell the family members about the new truths I'd found. They were not impressed—to say the least. They responded by giving me a lecture about the dangers of sneaking out and talking to "unbelievers." Reluctantly, I continued to live at the Unification Church, all the while, missing Marilyn and my real family.

Somehow, I did continue to read my Gideon Bible and work at Father Payton's Family Theater. Father Payton was a Roman Catholic priest who was, at one time, the Catholic equivalent of the Protestants' Billy Graham. Father Payton distributed professionally dramatized movies on the life of Christ. My job was to clean and maintain the films as they were rented to Catholic schools and various other places. Upon completion of my duties, I would sit for hours and hours watching the movies depicting the life of Christ.

God used the movies along with His Word continually to wash my mind as I read it to help me discern that the Unification Church was not teaching the *truth.* My devotion and love for Christ continued to run deep like a river. I finally decided to leave, which meant that I had to face the unpleasant task of telling Joseph who was discipling me that I was leaving the "family." As it turned out, after several months of oppression, I happily returned home even though I hadn't yet found my beloved Lord and Savior. *"By night on my bed I sought Him whom my soul loveth: I sought Him, but I found Him not"* (Song of

Solomon 3:1). A little more time would pass before I would find *"Him whom my soul loveth"* (Song of Solomon 3:4).

Father Payton had difficulty meeting the budget of the expensive office on Sunset Boulevard in Hollywood. I often saw him kneeling and praying before the statue of Mary asking her for the necessary funds for the weekly budget. I was amazed when the funds came through to the penny. He would often require all the staff members, including me, to meet for morning prayer at the foot of Mary. As I began to grow in Christ I became uncomfortable with this idolatrous practice. As it became more difficult to meet the budget, Father Payton cut back expenses and discharged me. I believe that my leaving was providential and that it kept me from false doctrine.

CHAPTER 14

Home Again

Upon returning home to my family and Marilyn, I secured a job at Henshey's department store in Santa Monica. I had become so confused and burnt-out over religion that I took a sabbatical from attending a church of any kind. However, my love for Christ remained unaltered. While I was working at Henshey's, two significant events took place.

The first event occurred during the Christmas season of 1969. I was working in the men's clothing department when a customer approached me and asked for a pair of socks. She told me that the socks were for her mother. I thought to myself, "How could this old lady have a mother when she looked like the 'Ancient of days"'herself? And, if she did have a mother, her mother would have to be well over one hundred years old."

The elderly lady proceeded to request that the socks not be too thick as her mother's feet would get too hot while in bed, nor be too thin as her feet would get too cold. "Brother! This sounds like Goldilocks and *The Three Bears* story," I thought to myself.

I have always been kind, respectful, and loving to the elderly, so I directed the lady to follow me over to the rack of socks. Like Goldilocks, I selected a pair that seemed "just right" and presented them to the woman. She examined the socks for a moment and then said, "No! No! These are too thin—they won't do at all."

I knew, right then, that I had a very unusual customer. After all, she had specified that she wanted *men's* socks for her mother. So, I patiently said, "Let's go to another department in the store where we have more sock racks and look there." She agreed and followed me.

I selected another pair of socks and handed them to her. She said, "These are *just right*." I was most glad, and I proceeded to write up a sales ticket for her when she asked me, "What is your name?"

Scarcely looking up, I told her, "Dick Wheeler." At the time, I was using the name Dick instead of Richard.

Then, out of the clear blue sky, she said, "Give!"

I looked up and said, "What?"

Again, she said, "Give!"

I didn't quite know what to think, so I asked, "Give what?"

She repeated, "Give!"

I acted somewhat dumbfounded and said, "Give money, help, time—myself?"

She nodded her head and said, "Yes, give."

I didn't want to pursue the direction of that conversation anymore since it didn't seem to be going anywhere and it was obvious that she was not asking me for a donation. I wrapped up the sale, and she left the store. About twenty minutes passed ,and I was alone in the lower end of the men's and boy's clothing section when, suddenly to my surprise, the elderly lady appeared again. I thought to myself, "Oh, no! She doesn't like the socks after all!"

But, instead, she said, "I thought I'd better give you something to help remind you to give." She reached into her purse, pulled out a one-dollar bill, and turned it over. On the dollar bill right next to "In God We Trust," she wrote the letter D for my name, Dick.

I thanked her for her kindness and the remembrance token. I wasn't blessed so much because she had given me a dollar (even back then a dollar didn't buy much). Rather, I was more blessed by the fact that she had taken the time to walk back (slowly, I might add) to reiterate her message to "give" and had given to me a token reminder which further impressed upon me the truth of her message.

"What is your name?" I asked.

"Pete," she replied.

"Pete?" I said, hoping she would explain her unusual name.

"Just Pete," she responded and then walked away.

I stared at the dollar and the position of the letter D that she had written. I thought about how unusual the lady and the whole encounter had been that day.

Suddenly, I remembered that, since it was the Christmas season, I could at least wish her "Merry Christmas." Our department had a door light tripper that rang a bell whenever someone walked across the light beam. Just as I had thought to wish Pete a "Merry Christmas," the doorbell chimed indicating that she had just stepped through the door. I turned to say "Merry Christmas" to her, but she was gone. She had disappeared. I hadn't been born-again at the time and knew nothing of the Bible verse that says, *"Be not forgetful to entertain strangers: for thereby some have entertained angels unawares"* (Hebrews 13:2).

I've never forgotten the lesson that Pete taught me of giving. As a matter of fact, that dollar became very special to me. I always carried it in my wallet to remind me to "give." I wouldn't have parted with that dollar, as poor as I was back then, for any amount of money that someone might have offered me. However, not long after my encounter with Pete, I was giving a troubled young man some guidance and recounted the story while showing him my special dollar. He was in great need of money at the time. I felt that the Lord was prompting me to give him the dollar and tell him how much I valued it. He was overwhelmed and blessed. I was less one dollar and blessed.

It is interesting to note that I have never been, even to this day, without a dollar to my name. The Lord has always provided for me as I have practiced the lesson of giving. I have benefitted much from the Bible and its principles on giving. Right after I was saved, I received teachings on tithing. Instead of making excuses about not having enough money or that my monthly expenses wouldn't allow me to tithe, I was foolish enough, in the eyes of the world, to give as I had learned. To date, the Lord has always met all my expenses. If you stop to think about it, God is the greatest Giver that humanity will ever know. What greater gift could He give us but His precious Son Jesus Christ to die for our sins? Would you give your child for the payment of sinners? I doubt it. Yet, *"...God so loved the world, that He gave His only begotten Son, that whosoever believeth in Him should not perish, but have everlasting life"* (John 3:16).

The second significant event that occurred while I was working at Henshey's came as a result of meeting a fellow employee named Shelly. She told me about a new way of life called Nichiren Shoshu. It was a religion involving chanting for whatever a person wished or desired. She gave me the chant formula, and I began practicing it in earnest for an audition I had scheduled in Hollywood. The audition was for a professional musical to be held for tourists in Jackson Hole, Wyoming, during the summer months. I had done well on my previous singing and acting auditions, but on this particular day's audition, I had to demonstrate my dancing ability in front of comedian Carol Burnett's personal choreographer. In order for you to appreciate the amount of anxiety I was feeling regarding my dance audition, let me tell you about my theater dancing ability, or better yet, the lack of it.

While studying for the theater, I had several opportunities to receive dance instruction from professional theater dancers. During class instruction, Paul, my instructor, constantly took me aside to tell me that I was the worst dancer he had ever seen. He told me that I had no sense of rhythm and that I was a total klutz. He advised me to get out of musical comedy acting because it involved a lot of dancing. Seeing my disappointment, he suggested that I take private tap dancing lessons from his friend since, sometimes, people with my problem could learn rhythm by learning tap dance.

I showed up for my first private lesson, and I tap danced to whatever I was told by my new instructor. After the session, the instructor took me aside and said, "You're the worst dancer I've ever seen." He echoed the words that Paul had told me, "Get out of musical theater, because it involves too much dancing."

With that as a background, I hope you can appreciate my anxiety over dancing for Carol Burnett's choreographer. I knew that I was facing a *HUGE* obstacle to my final audition for being selected—or being rejected—for my first paid musical. I was sweating it out, to say the least, so I resorted to my new chanting formula that Shelly had given me. I remember she had told me, "Chant for whatever you desire, and you will receive it." I chanted all the way from Santa Monica to Hollywood—a forty-minute drive.

I recall entering a room full of would- be performers who were looking for a chance to be selected for the summer stock musical. The choreographer stepped into the room and took about six of us at a time. He had a clipboard listing each of our names and a place to score our dancing ability. He demonstrated the particular dance movement he wanted us to copy, so he could score us. We began the small routine he gave us, and, all the while, I was chanting under my breath in hopes that I was doing all right. After we finished, he politely thanked us all and said, "Don't call us—we'll call you." I walked out feeling indifferent and without knowing, either good or bad, how I did.

About two weeks later, I was performing with a small acting group for a women's club in Beverly Hills when I received a phone call from the producer and director of the summer stock theater company. He told me that I was hired to take the leading role in the musical. I was shocked, but I almost had a heart attack when he told me that I scored as one of the highest in the dancing category! After gaining my composure, I calmly said, "Are you sure you have the right person, because I am a terrible dancer."
"Yes," he said. Then he gave me the date to show up for the job in Jackson Hole, Wyoming.

I thought to myself, "This chanting must really work." I didn't know about the powers of demonic influence. However, I soon learned that there are *always* strings attached to evil powers and whatever they grant.

CHAPTER 15

I'm Gonna Be a Star

Like a starry-eyed child, I innocently said good-bye to my family and Marilyn, so I could travel down the road to fame and glory, or so I thought. I had a contract to perform for four and a half months and would return home in the early part of September. I hitched a ride with a hired actress who attended the same drama school. Upon our arrival, she was taken to a cabin where all the girls stayed. I was placed in an old trailer that had all the trimmings of the 1950s corny blonde paneling look. The trailer was destined to house four of eight male actors, and another trailer would accommodate the remaining four actors.

We began rehearsing our musical, and I quickly discovered the evil web that was attached to my chanting. Of the twelve males on the cast of actors, and the director, pianist, and set designers, nine of them were homosexuals! I had nowhere to turn. With a signed contract, I was trapped and totally disillusioned. Mentally, I had to escape. So, I got into Zen Buddhism, and continued astrology, while reading the New Testament. Needless to say I was messed up. At the time I didn't know God's promise:

"But if from thence thou shalt seek the LORD thy God, thou shalt find Him, if thou seek Him with all thy heart and with all thy soul. When thou art in tribulation, and all these things are come upon thee, even in the latter days, if thou turn to the LORD thy God, and shalt be obedient unto His voice; (For the LORD thy God is a merciful God;) He

will not forsake thee, neither destroy thee, nor forget the covenant of thy fathers which He sware unto them" (Deuteronomy 4:29-31).

After rehearsals and our second daily performance, I physically escaped to Wyoming's mountains in Big Hole Valley. It was a beautiful place to live that offered former rendezvous scenes of by-gone days. That summer, I'd say that I was in Heaven but without Christ, especially since I was stuck performing in a musical for the entire summer with lost, perverted, debauched, and godless people who desperately needed salvation. To make matters worse, I wasn't in any spiritual condition to offer them an alternative. It was hell on earth, so I continued to read my Bible and pray to Jesus.

Another obvious folly about my chanting was that I still couldn't dance even though I had been selected as the winner of the dancing auditions. It became very apparent in a somewhat humorous way. During the very first day of our rehearsals, Tim, the choreographer, began to position our dance movements for the production. Since I had the leading part, I was required to be in the center of all the action and dance throughout the entire stage performance.

As Tim began to direct me to move and dance about the stage, he suddenly stopped and asked, "Is this the best you can dance?"

"Yes," I answered honestly.

Tim left the stage and went down to where Dave, the director, sat viewing the first rehearsal. After consulting for a few moments, Dave asked me to step forward to the apron of the stage and said, "I thought you could dance."

"I'm the worst dancer in history," I said.

"That's what Tim just told me!" Dave replied.

To solve the problem, they creatively had to block the two productions around me to appear as though I weren't supposed to be dancing.

That summer did bring me some dear friends who worked at various business establishments around the city of Jackson Hole. Ralph and Tomi Wolff owned the Rock Hound Paradise Shop that was located near the Pink Garter Theater where I worked. They took me to a local community Bible church on Sunday mornings, which afforded me my first experience with a Christian Protestant church. I enjoyed being with Ralph and Tomi who were in their early fifties. Tomi's mother, Sue, worked and lived with them during the tourist season. As a family, they extended Christian love to me which gave me hope and a sense of security. Especially, since I was homesick and longing for my dear family back in Santa Monica, California.

Spiritually, I was still as lost as ever, but I was unaware of my condition. If someone had asked me if I was a Christian, I would have answered, "most certainly." At that time in my life, I didn't have the foggiest notion of what salvation meant and, tragically, I thought I was a Christian.

At the end of my summer's work, I was so deceived, spiritually, that I had purposed in my heart to consult an astrologer on my way home from Jackson Hole. I was going to inquire of a well-known astrologer in Salt Lake City as to whether or not Marilyn and I should marry. I wanted to know if the stars would show favor towards Marilyn's astrological sign and mine. Fortunately, I wasn't able to meet with the astrologer because my connecting flight in Salt Lake City was too tightly scheduled, time wise, to allow me the opportunity of taking a taxi into the city and still be able to catch my flight to Los Angeles.

Thanks to our merciful Savior Jesus Christ, I would soon learn that *"there is a God in heaven that revealeth secrets, and maketh known to the king . . . what shall be in the latter days . . . and He that revealeth secrets maketh known to thee what shall come to pass . . ."* (Daniel 2:28-29).

CHAPTER 16

The Eavesdropper Gets Saved

After returning home from my summer acting job, I had a joyful reunion with my family and friends. By this time, Marilyn and I were very much committed to each other. Thus, we became engaged and made our wedding plans for the following summer. We set our wedding date for July 29, 1972. The only major hindrance to our relationship was in spiritual matters, as we couldn't agree on which religion we would practice. Marilyn quickly figured out that I was in major spiritual turmoil. We spent untold hours going around and around about Biblical principles that meant so much to me but so little to her. Usually, we ended up crying together and I would apologize for being such a crazy religious basket case.

Marilyn and I began taking classes together at Santa Monica College. One of our classes was called *Family and Marriage*. After one of our class sessions, our instructor, Carol Karlin, asked Marilyn and me if we would like to attend a Bible study in her home. We agreed and attended our first Bible study. I don't remember what the topic or particular teaching was that night, but I do remember that, afterwards, I turned to one of Marilyn's other college instructors, Tru Mullenhoff, and asked her to please speak to Marilyn about Christianity. I explained to Tru that every time Marilyn and I tried to discuss it, we ended up in an argument. I decided to leave the room so that my presence wouldn't intimidate Marilyn. As I waited in another room which was within hearing range, I wondered, "What in

God's earth could Tru say to Marilyn that I could not or had not told her about Christ?"

I could hear Tru reading the little booklet called *The Four Spiritual Laws* to Marilyn. As she read, I was all ears. I had never before heard that people were born spiritually dead and that they must be "born again" by inviting and receiving Christ into their hearts to be Lord and Savior of their lives. *"...Verily, verily, I say unto thee, Except a man be born again, he cannot see the kingdom of God. ...Except a man be born of water and of the Spirit, he cannot enter into the kingdom of God. That which is born of the flesh is flesh; and that which is born of the Spirit is spirit"* (John 3:3-6).

As Tru shared the plan of salvation with Marilyn, I realized that, in all my religious experiences of Roman Catholicism, Mormonism, Jehovah's Witnesses, Moonies, Nichiren Shoshu, Zen Buddhism, astrology, and Herbert W. Armstrongism, I had *never* heard the simple plan of salvation.

"Do you want to invite Christ into your life?" Tru asked Marilyn.

"I don't know how to pray," responded Marilyn.

"I will pray out loud, and you can repeat after me, if you'd like," said Tru.

"That would be fine," answered Marilyn.

As Tru began to lead Marilyn in the prayer, I found myself repeating the words. I realized that I was a sinner and that I needed to trust Christ as my Savior in order to please God—apart from any works of self-righteousness that I could ever perform.

Amazingly, the week before, I had been kneeling before my bed in my small apartment, distraught over the knowledge that I couldn't do anything else to please God.

In prayer, I had told God that I was quitting—giving up any efforts in trying to please Him. I had cried in frustration, surrendering my will and efforts to Christ. I had been utterly exhausted from the many years of seeking God and not getting any closer to Him. I had gotten up off my knees and flopped myself onto the bed and fallen into the deepest sleep I had ever recalled experiencing. I had felt dead to the world, and I had slept and slept. I remember trying to wake up, but I had felt as though there was a hand on my chest that kept me pinned down to the bed. Every time I had tried to rise, it was impossible. Whatever or whoever was holding me down was stronger than my will and ability to rise up. I felt that I had heard the still, small voice of the Lord reassuring me that all was well and that He was not yet finished with me.

I had yielded to Him and fallen back into a deep sleep again. Sometime later, I had tried to rise again, but I was still pinned to the bed by an invisible hand on my chest. Encountering no fear, I again submitted to the working of the Lord. I never before, nor have I since, experienced such an occurrence. I can only surmise that the Lord was doing a supernatural work within my fallen and perplexed spirit. Perhaps the Lord had been preparing my spirit for the night of the Bible study where I heard the plan of salvation, so I could respond to the calling of Christ with ears to hear and eyes to see. *"But blessed are your eyes, for they see: and your ears, for they hear"* (Matthew 13:16).

It was as if God was patiently waiting all those years for me to reach the end of my rope in trying to gain His merit and favor with works. Now that my will was out of the way, His will could take over. The Lord will not allow man to glory in himself, for man is to glory in Him. He is to receive all glory and honor for the good and righteousness accomplished in one's life.

"For by grace are ye saved through faith; and that not of yourselves: it is the gift of God: Not of works, lest any man should boast [glory]. *For we are His workmanship, created in Christ Jesus unto good works, which God hath before ordained that we should walk in them"* (Ephesians 2:8-10).

As I prayed the sinner's prayer with Tru and Marilyn from another room, Christ, in His infinite power, cleansed me by His atoning blood that He shed on the cross at Calvary and filled me with His love. I was made whiter than snow.

"Have mercy upon me, O God, according to thy lovingkindness: according unto the multitude of thy tender mercies blot out my transgressions. Wash me thoroughly from mine iniquity, and cleanse me from my sin. For I acknowledge my transgressions: and my sin is ever before me . . . Behold, thou desirest truth in the inward parts: and in the hidden part thou shalt make me to know wisdom. Purge me with hyssop, and I shall be clean: **wash me, and I shall be whiter than snow**. *Make me to hear joy and gladness; that the bones which thou hast broken may rejoice. Hide thy face from my sins, and blot out all mine iniquities. Create in me a clean heart, O God; and renew a right spirit within me. Cast me not away from thy presence; and take not thy Holy Spirit from me. Restore unto me the joy of thy salvation; and uphold me with thy*

free [willing] *spirit. Then will I teach transgressors thy ways; and sinners shall be converted unto thee"* (Psalm 51:1-13).

I remember saying, "Amen," in unison with Tru and Marilyn. Marilyn and I were supernaturally "born again." I felt free and light-hearted. Everything seemed clear. I was released from a huge burden that I had carried on my back for such a long time. Many years later, I came to know the story of *Pilgrim's Progress* by John Bunyan. I could reflect and identify with Christian and what it must have meant to him to look up at the cross of Calvary and lose his burden. I, too, lost my burden. It contained the demonic spirit of religion and the false notion that *my* efforts gained God's acceptance. My eyes had been enlightened that it was *His* unmerited favor that only *He* gives, which is *His* free gift of grace.

I walked back into the room where Tru and Marilyn were seated. We were all wiping the cleansing tears of salvation from our faces. Marilyn realized I had been saved in the same moment she received Christ as her Lord and Savior.

One week after we had received our salvation, we were baptized in the ocean at Laguna Beach, California. It was March of 1972 during the height of the "Jesus Movement." It just so happened that Marilyn's teacher, Carol Karlin, had a husband who was a Messianic Hebrew. Bob Karlin shared his desire for me to grow in Christ, so he invited me to attend a Bible study that was taught by a man named Hal Lindsey. Hal was teaching from his new book, *The Late Great Planet Earth,* to a group of businessmen on Tuesday mornings. The focus of the teaching was about the imminent return of Jesus Christ.

I had an insatiable hunger for God's Word, and I wanted to grow as much as possible in the grace and knowledge of Christ. Hal recognized my desire and, after breakfast one morning, he invited me to become a student at a Bible school that he and several other Bible teachers had opened. The school, called the Light and Power House, was located just outside the university campus of UCLA in Westwood Village, California. Hal didn't have to ask twice. Immediately, I enrolled and began to study the Bible diligently. Spiritually, I grew more in those two years of Bible teaching than I had grown in all the previous years of my life. I continued to sing professionally and worked full-time at a company I started called Maranatha Roofing.

Marilyn received Bible training and discipleship from Bev Counts, the wife of one of the instructors at our Bible school. Just as our lives had been miraculously transformed, so was our relationship to each. We were in love and preparing for a life as husband and wife. I was completely immersed in learning about and seeking the Kingdom of Heaven. *"Seek ye first the kingdom of God, and His righteousness; and all these things shall be added unto you"* (Matthew 6:33).

In fact, during that time, I spent so much time learning about His divine love and grace that my interest in guns, knives, hunting, and skinning were all put on the back burner. It was a special season of my life wherein God was preparing me for ministry, a ministry that, at the time, I did not know was hidden within the secret counsel of my Heavenly Father.

CHAPTER 17

A Religious Fanatic

By 1976, I had obtained extensive Bible training under the teaching of Hal Lindsey and other former lesser-known Dallas Theological Seminary professors who were living in Southern California. While sitting under the teachings of Hal, I began to develop a spiritual imbalance. All I sought and lived for was the Second Coming of Jesus Christ. I had, what could be termed, "rapture fever." Every current event that was of significance and which pointed to the coming of Jesus Christ left me elated. Earthquakes and various other disasters caused me to get excited and to *"look up"* for my "redemption draweth near" (Luke 21:28). I was certain that Christ's return to earth to judge the world of sin and set up His Kingdom was just around the corner.

During the 1970s, many evangelicals were "rapture struck." Millions of Christians and non-Christians alike bought Hal Lindsay's book, *The Late Great Planet Earth.* In fact, it was the number-one nonfiction bestseller of the 1970s. Hundreds of people were coming to Christ in anticipation of His Second Coming. I got to the point where I actually looked forward to calamities. I was what I would call an optimistic pessimist.

Up to this point, as you've read my life testimony, you probably have figured out that I demonstrate an extremist personality which goes hog-wild and is overly zealous in whatever I pursue. So, naturally, as a Christian, I was zealous for Christ. Someone once told me that new

Christians were "cage cases" and that they should be locked up until they learn the Bible well enough to become Biblically balanced. I was out of control and went crazy by sharing Christ and His Second Coming with everyone I met.

As an example, I acquired a part-time job as a noon activity director at a local public school in Culver City, California. My job was to keep an eye on the first-through sixth-grade children during lunch, which allowed the teachers an opportunity to have a peaceful lunch—away from the children. The fourth-through sixth-graders kept me very busy, as they were a wild bunch who terrorized the campus. Fights broke out daily. I began to isolate and remove the problem children by "benching" them. During their bench time, I shared the love of Jesus with them. Since they were benched with no place to go to get into mischief, they gladly listened as I told them Bible stories. It didn't take very long for the school bullies to begin telling their friends, "Mr. Wheeler is cool." Every day, rather than playing, large crowds of children gathered around me to hear more Bible stories from the Old and New Testament. The teachers began noticing that the difficult students were behaving well in class and at recess time. Their behavior was so good that the teachers couldn't believe their eyes.

Daily, I prayed with the students to receive Christ as their Lord and Savior. I finished working that school year and returned the following year to begin where I had left off. The children could hardly wait to return to school that year so they could hear more Bible stories and share their faith with me. By the middle of the new school year, the entire campus was like a church Sunday school. The teachers hadn't realized what was going on because they had been *inside* eating in the teacher's lunchroom while I was *outside* with the children.

My days of joy suddenly ended and so did my job when the principal called me into her office. She asked me, "Are you handing out little pocket Bibles to the children?"

"Yes," I answered.

"You can't do that! It's forbidden by the state," she replied. She further explained, "Jewish children are getting all excited and are telling their parents that they have received Christ as their Messiah!"

You can only surmise how well the knowledge of my actions was received, especially, since the principal, herself, was Jewish. However, she did recognize the value of having me on campus and the resulting peace that had swept over the campus.

"Will you promise to keep your mouth closed about the Bible and anything of a religious nature?" she asked.

I was sold out for Christ! I couldn't give my consent! The result was that she proceeded to terminate me on the spot.

Besides being in hot water with the public school system, I was in trouble with Marilyn's dad, Mr. Cobb, who was an avowed atheist. He found it most disconcerting that his youngest daughter had gotten mixed up with a "religious fanatic." We had many heated discussions about Christ, ending with neither of us convincing the other of his personal persuasions.

However, over the four years that I dated Marilyn, Mr. Cobb and I grew to love each other in spite of our religious differences. He, being a Scottish immigrant and a lover of history, taught me many wonderful things and shared his experiences working in Britain during World War II. He was a very hard-working individual whose example taught me the importance of hard work, diligence, and saving money.

Like Earl Brent, the Lord used Mr. Cobb to help train me to become a useful and skilled handyman who would be in good stead as a someday homeowner and a "honey-do-fix-this-for-me" husband to Marilyn.

CHAPTER 18

Unto Us a Child Is Born

Finally, on September 27, 1976, I became more down-to-earth as the result of an event that changed my life. In Hollywood, California, our first child, Noelle, came into the world. Wow! What a life-changing experience that was! I was a father. Being a dad caused me to become more responsible. When I read or heard of disasters and political corruption, I became angry and concerned. All I could think was, "How dare those politicians vote that way! They're destroying my country!" Being a father, I felt compelled to protect my daughter from corruption of all sorts.

It is interesting to note that until I had a child, I didn't care a whit about my country. All I cared about was, "When is the Rapture coming?" I was a conservative voter, but that was about the extent of my political involvement regarding America. I felt that Christians were of another world, that being Heaven. I was so "heavenly minded that I was no earthly good." I actually got to the point where I wanted America to fail so that the Lord would hurry up and come back to earth to establish His reign.

By the time Noelle was two years old, I was convinced that America was in a pitiful condition. To me, America looked as if it was beyond hope of ever being restored to its days of strong Biblical moorings. Thus, I decided to do the next best thing—flee to the mountains to protect my baby girl and wife. We packed up everything, lock, stock, and barrel, so we could move to Port Orford, which is on the southern coast of Oregon.

Port Orford had 1,060 inhabitants and offered the best of two worlds. First, it afforded me the opportunity to live in a primitive environment where bears, elk, deer, racoon, and a variety of other critters lived. For a Davy Crockett loving mountain man like myself, it suited me just fine. As for Marilyn, she, like a good wife, followed without much complaint and went along loving and supporting me, a half touched nut. Another good reason to move to Port Orford was the town offered us a safe place to live while we awaited Christ's Second Coming, a sort of escape mentality.

CHAPTER 19

Do Not Despise the Day of Small Beginnings

Immediately upon arriving in Port Orford, I began to look for a good Christian church in which to raise my family. Being such a small town, Port Orford had only three Protestant churches. The Lutheran, Community, and Assemblies of God Church. I tried the local Community Church and found it to be as "dead as a door nail." The people were not friendly, and they took no notice of new faces in the crowd. I pondered, "How could we go unnoticed in a church of seventy-five souls?"

I was left with no alternative except to try the local Assemblies of God church. Keep in mind that my Bible seminary training was non-Pentecostal. In fact, it was hostile toward the Pentecostal school of thought. I was taught dispensational theology from professors of Dallas Theological Seminary. Every Biblical doctrine that I was taught fit into neat little teachings that had a plan and a purpose. I was taught that the nine spiritual gifts, as related in I Corinthians 12, were unnecessary and obsolete upon the Bible's written completion and the establishment of the church of Jesus Christ. Modern tongue-speaking Pentecostal religion with all its "signs and wonders" was erroneous and deceptive. I was taught to believe that it bordered on being "of the devil."

As you can imagine, I was very scared and filled with anxiety when we entered the Pentecostal church. But, to my amazement, the people were actually friendly and warm. They even welcomed us to Port Orford. Pastor Mike Hodges embraced us with open arms. We made several visits to the church and spent some considerable time getting acquainted with Pastor Mike and his family. Pastor Mike recognized my knowledge of God's Word and my desire to serve and minister. Thus, he encouraged me to continue to study for the ministry by taking further Bible training through the Assemblies of God correspondence course.

I was hungry for as much of God's Word as I could get, so I enrolled in the program. Through hard work and diligence, I eventually finished the course and became ordained to preach.

One of the first ministries that I plunged into was our church's Royal Rangers. The nearest way to describe the Royal Rangers is to say that it is much like the Boy Scouts of America. The difference is that, the emphasis is not only on outdoor camping skills but also on Bible memorization and activities that will promote a desire for boys to love and serve Christ as they grow into manhood. Royal Rangers are, basically, Christian Boy Scouts.

I loved every minute of the program, and I could hardly wait for our once-a-week meeting. The boys and I hit it off with a great start since I was "touched in the head" with the love of adventure, mountain men, trapping, skinning, hunting, and all the other "wild and crazy" things most boys naturally love. Within three months of arriving in Port Orford, the Royal Rangers had planned a powwow at Camp Farragut, Idaho. Anything to do with camping suited me just fine. So, of course, I kissed my wife and two-year-old daughter, Noelle, good-bye. Then I headed north for a four-day camping trip with Senior Commander Gary Doran along with about twelve boys, ages ten through sixteen.

After setting up camp, we had some free time on our hands to check out the area. When I looked up, much to my amazement, there were tents as far as the eye could see. It looked like a Civil War encampment. I'd never seen so many pitched tents together in all my born days. It was glorious! I was such a greenhorn to the Royal Rangers that, for some reason, I had the impression that they were a ministry that had only been initiated by our church. I didn't realize that the Royal Rangers was a national program with thousands of members throughout the U.S.A. and many other parts of the world. While surveying the encampment, I quickly spied, above the tent line, the towering tops of tipis. I meandered my way toward them, all the while wondering, "What in the world are tipis doing here amongst the Royal Rangers?" As I cleared the last row of tents, I came upon the most beautiful sight my Davy Crockett mind could have imagined. There before my eyes, I beheld grown men and older boys dressed in buckskins, fur hats of various sorts, and colorful calico 1850s styled shirts. They were throwing tomahawks and knives, skinning varmints, and chewing buffalo jerky. There were trappers sitting around a huge fire pit jawing about their various exploits of shooting black powder rifles.

Suddenly, about fifteen yards behind me, I heard the roar and thunder of several black powder rifles fire off. Surprised, I jumped and then pinched myself to make sure it was all real, because I was almost positive that I had died and gone to Heaven. It was definitely my idea and dream of what Heaven would be like.

After gaining my composure so as not to appear too starry-eyed, I approached a heavy bearded mountain man clad in buckskin and asked him, "Say stranger, who are all you guys? Are you pagans that just so happen to be sharing the same camp facility with us Royal Rangers?"

He looked at me strangely and then, eyeing me from head-to-toe and seeing that I was in my Royal Ranger uniform, said, "Why fellow Ranger, don't ya know, man? This *is* the Royal Rangers!"

In amazement, I said, *"It is?!* How do you get to become a part of *this*?"

He proceeded to explain to me the proper steps required to be initiated into the Fellowship Camping Fraternity which they called FCF. He told me that after I completed and passed the proper leadership training courses, I could become a part of the fraternity of buck skinners in the FCF in the Oregon district where I lived. I thanked him and shook his hand. In a daze, I strolled out of the camp.

I could hardly imagine or believe that there was such a Christian 1850s trapping fraternity and that I could become a part of it in my own state! I was overcome with emotion. I looked up to heaven and thanked my Heavenly Father for directing my steps to move to Oregon and learn about the Royal Rangers. The Lord began speaking to my heart in that still, small voice and said, "This program will launch your ministry. You will travel throughout the United States and become an evangelist proclaiming my Good News to all I send you to. I want you to make four outfits— a mountain man, Indian, cowboy, and Pilgrim outfit. Wait upon Me to open doors for you to further the Gospel. For this you were born. When people thought you were retarded or stupid, I was only preparing you for My service. It was

I who formed you in the womb and created you in the secret place. All the skills you have learned—hunting, roping, quick draw, hawk and knife throwing and all the books you've ever read on the Old West—I will use to weave into Bible stories and truths that you will share with young people. As you use these gifts and talents, I will reveal My plan and purpose for their lives in the same unique way that I have created and molded you."

The Lord stopped speaking, and I burst into tears. Finally, I realized *why* I was "a retarded gopher trapper." It had taken the Lord twenty-three years to reveal this to me. I understood that the Lord had created me and directed my life in a special way for His purpose. To the world I looked like a failure, but to God I was a diamond in the rough.

"For ye see your calling, brethren, how that not many wise men after the flesh, not many mighty, not many noble, are called: But God hath chosen the foolish things of the world to confound the wise; and God hath chosen the weak things of the world to confound the things which are mighty . . . That no flesh should glory in His presence" (I Corinthians 1:26-29).

The following summer in 1979, at the age of thirty-one, I was initiated into the Fellowship Camping Fraternity and received the name "Little Bear" as my frontier pen name.

CHAPTER 20

Our Dream Home

When we arrived in Port Orford during the spring of 1978, we bought our first home. We paid a whopping $7,500 for a little shack which was just a hop, skip, and a jump from the beach. If you could imagine what a $7,500 house looks like, your imagination probably wouldn't be too far off. Half of the windows were held together by the paint on the dry rotted wood. If we pushed too hard on a window, it would fall out. It was fun to play marbles on the floor because the marbles would naturally roll out away from our hands. In many places throughout the house, if we had stepped down too hard, we could have found ourselves falling through the floor to the ground below. The dark and dingy shower stall was spotted with black mold, and the concrete shower floor was laid precariously upon the rotted floor joist. Taking a shower in those conditions greatly improved our prayer life!

During the night, we would wake up to the sound of rats gnawing on the wood trying to eat their way into the house through the rotting floors. One particular evening, just after we had settled down to sleep, I was dreaming that a rat crawled up my arm and then rested upon my chest. Startled, I woke up. Lo and behold, when I opened my eyes in the full moon-lit bedroom, I could see that my dream was a reality! A rat *was* resting on my arm and staring me right in the face! I could see its beady little eyes and whiskers. I let out a yell and threw up my arms, tossing the rat against the wall. I was still half asleep and was wondering if I was just having a dream or if it really did happen to me. Remaining on my back with my heart beating a mile a minute, I could see, out of the corner of my eye, a rat on my white reading pillow which was lying on the floor next to me. *Now*, I definitely knew that it was *not* a nightmare!

I sat up in my bed and, although I still wasn't totally coherent, grabbed my bedroom slipper. I clutched it in my hand to protect my wife and myself should the rat appear again. Since I was only half-awake, try as I might to stay awake, I dozed back to sleep. Shamefully, I slept at my post with a dangerous and, perhaps, rabid rat in my house.

I don't recall how much time had transpired, but I was awakened again by a feeling of tiny feet walking toward my face. Again, I let out a slight yell, so as not to awaken Marilyn, and threw my slipper toward the attacking rat. I was now fully awake and shaken. I got up to turn on the table lamp that was next to my bed and wondered what in the world was going on. Slightly stirring, Marilyn asked, "What is wrong?"

I answered, "Oh, nothing much. I just think there is a rat around here." I didn't want to alarm her.

While I pondered what I should do next, I spied the rat re-entering the bedroom from underneath the bedroom door, which was shaved quite high from the floor. I couldn't believe my eyes! That rat had the nerve to approach our bed—right before my eyes! I just knew that the rat was mentally deranged. No rat in its right mind would be so bold as to approach a human in brightly lit conditions. No bones about it, it was going to be the rat or me. One of us had to go. The house certainly wasn't big enough for both of us. The rat was itching for a showdown, and I was more than ready. After all, was I a man or a "mouse?

As I started to leave the bed to move toward the rat, it scurried back out the way it came in. By this time, Marilyn was fully awakened. I told her, "There is a rat in the house, and it is determined to get me!"

Naturally, she panicked and got out of bed saying, "I'm heading for the living room."

"You won't be safe in there, because the rat is somewhere outside of our bedroom," I warned her.

I thought of a plan. I just knew, sooner or later, that demented rat would be coming back into the room to get me. So, without a motion, I waited by the closed door in order to ambush the varmint. Slowly, I opened the bedroom door, which led into the kitchen, where I happened to spot a broom right next to the refrigerator. I took it in hand, went back to my station, closed the door, and patiently waited. It wasn't very long before the rat crawled underneath the door and headed right back toward the bed.

"Now I've got you, you dirty, little rat! This place ain't big enough for the both of us," I yelled, putting on my John Wayne impersonation.

Marilyn chuckled in half fear. The rat saw that I had blocked its way of escape and that it was trapped with a family's best rat 'n' mouse killer in hand—a BROOM! The rat high-tailed it under the bed while Marilyn high-tailed it to the living room couch for safety, away from the dangerous attacking rat.

"Lift up the bedcovers so I can see where the rat is positioned," I told her before she retreated.

I lay down on the floor, on my belly, with a flashlight in hand so I could see the underside of the bed. The rat was by the back wheel of the bedframe planning its escape, I was sure.

My dilemma was, "How am I gonna approach that rat? If I go to one side, it will escape by running to the other as fast as lightning. As long as I am lying on the floor at the foot of the bed, it can't get past me alive."

For a moment, I just stayed there thinking. Then, all of a sudden, I came up with a brilliant plan. I could shoot the critter! The only problem was that I didn't want to blow a hole in the side of the house. I already had enough holes in the house, and I certainly didn't need anymore. But wait! I remembered that I had a six-shooter BB gun that could kill a rat and not penetrate a wall, so I called out to Marilyn, "Get my BB gun out of the den and bring it to me."

She tiptoed into the room and handed her brave husband the BB gun and then hastily retreated back to the living room. I placed the butt of the gun on the carpet. Realizing that I would have only one opportunity for a good shot, I knew that I *had* to make my shot count! I took deliberate and careful aim and then squeezed the trigger. POP! went the air gun. The rat jumped up and hit its head on the bedframe and then darted behind the nightstand to lick its wounds.

My only chance for another shot at the now bloodshot and wounded, perhaps even rabid, rat was if it happened to be dumb enough to run from behind the nightstand to the opposite wall. Sure enough, as I peeked toward the wall, I saw the rat at the very front of the nightstand. Before the rat could whistle "hickory, dickory, dock," I emptied my revolver's last five shots. The rat keeled over and had the decency to die on an old tissue that had slipped down to the floor alongside the nightstand days before. The battle of "rabid rat" was over! I had protected my family and home and had never been so proud in all my life.

I shot many animals over the years, but conquering that demented rat was the most exciting bit of hunting action I have ever experienced. I would have taken that rat to the taxidermist if I hadn't been stone broke and couldn't afford such a luxury.

The following morning, I crawled underneath the house and plugged every hole where a mouse or a rat could break through. Over a period of months after that episode, I had two more shoot-outs to rid our home of rats.

As bad as that house may have seemed to be to you, my reader, it was our first home, and we were very proud of it. The Lord provided us with the time and the money to fix it up and, over the years, it became very precious to us.

"But I rejoiced in the Lord greatly. . . . Not that I speak in respect of want: for I have learned, in whatsoever state I am, therewith to be content. I know both how to be abased, and I know how to abound: every where and in all things I am instructed both to be full and to be hungry, both to abound and to suffer need. I can do all things through Christ which strengtheneth me" (Philippians 4:10-13).

CHAPTER 21

A Fisher of Fish

We were blessed by having dear friends from our former Bible school days wish us a warm welcome upon our arrival in Port Orford, Oregon. Early in our Christian walk, the Lord had given us Dick and Meg Burkett who were very special instruments used of God in our lives. Dick was a fisherman who owned his own commercial fishing boat. Since I had arrived in Oregon during the summer salmon season, Dick hired me on as a salmon puller. Work was scarce in that small town of 1,060 people, so I was more than happy to be employed. I thought it was going to be a fun job—fishing all day long pulling in salmon by the hundreds. I soon learned differently. There were days we would fish from 6:00 a.m. until 9:00 p.m. and would return to shore with not a single saleable fish. I learned the value and depth of what Peter must have felt when, after fishing all night, he and the disciples hadn't caught anything (John 21:4-6).

However, at other times, there were so many fish that fishing was hard work. In addition to actually fishing, there were sundry chores: scrubbing, baiting hooks, and organizing gear—all the while, sitting in the sun getting cooked. Cloudy days were a welcome relief, although they often brought storms.

I remember one storm in particular. I thought it would be my last storm of life and that I would die at sea which, for a "land lubber" like me, was a terrible way to die. The wind had increased to such a fury that it began to create waves that made a roller coaster ride look like kiddyland rides. Dick recognized that the conditions were becoming dangerous. Calmly, he said, "Get into the two-man cabin and head for home."

He did *not* have to ask me twice! I got into the cabin and hung on for dear life. We were pitched up-and-down and back-and-forth like a cork on the water. I was hanging on so tightly that I noticed my knuckles were blanched as white as snow. There was a small window next to me out of which, at one moment, I would see nothing but gray sky and, in the next moment, when the boat reeled to the left, all I could see was water. All of this was happening while ascending and descending huge violent waves much like on a roller coaster. I personally related to Psalm 107:23-31:

> *"They that go down to the sea in ships, that do business in great waters; These see the works of the LORD, and his wonders in the deep. For He commandeth, and raiseth the stormy wind, which lifteth up the waves thereof. They mount up to the heaven, they go down again to the depths: their soul is melted because of trouble. They reel to and fro, and stagger like a drunken man, and are at their wit's end. Then they cry unto the Lord in their trouble, and He bringeth them out of their distresses. He maketh the storm a calm, so that the waves thereof are still. Then are they glad because they be quiet; so He bringeth them unto their desired haven.*

Oh that men would praise the LORD for His goodness, and for His wonderful works to the children of men!"

Obviously, I lived to tell the tale, but I was an extremely happy fisherman when the salmon season came to a close and I eagerly sought a new profession—on land! I told myself, "Let's see. Jesus called fishermen into ministry—what other profession did He call in? I know! I can be a carpenter just like Jesus."

By this time, we had become friends with a wonderful family, Steve and Carol Phillips. Steve was a craftsman boat builder, and he offered me a job building boats. I was delighted to be a carpenter and immediately went to work for him. Our friendship blossomed in spite of my lack of carpentry skills. I had been working with Steve for a year when he came up to me one day and asked me to come outside the shop to have a talk with him. We strolled out back and sat down. Steve put his hand on my shoulder and, in a loving, kind and gentle way, said, "Richard, you are the worst carpenter I have ever worked with, and I am such a perfectionist that I can't handle sending boats out of my shop that may sink as a result of your work."

I knew Steve was right, but it came as a complete surprise to me. *"Faithful are the wounds of a friend"* (Proverb: 27:6). I got teary-eyed. Steve tried to comfort me by telling me that he had been observing me and had found in all manners of my life, including work and church, that I didn't do well at anything I set my hands to except preaching. He further explained that he believed the Lord was calling me to full-time ministry and that I should pursue serving the Lord on a full-time basis.

With that revelation, my only dilemma was "How is the church going to afford me? It's already having difficulties meeting the senior pastor's monthly budget and is stretching itself by giving me a part-time salary of $25 each month."

The church's goal was to increase my salary by $25 every three months until I reached a livable wage. All I could think was, "How does an unemployed husband with a wife, child, and one-on-the-way support a family on $25 a month?"

My circumstances left me with only pure blind faith, as it was impossible by sight. I knew it, and Steve knew it. In fact, the whole church knew it, but someone forgot to tell God. I decided to take God for His Word and trust Him to perform it.

"But my God shall supply all your need according to His riches in glory by Christ Jesus" (Philippians 4:19).

"Trust in the Lord with all thine heart; and lean not unto thine own understanding. In all thy ways acknowledge Him, and He shall direct thy paths" (Proverbs 3:5-6).

CHAPTER 22

Fisher of Men

Immediately after Steve dismissed me, I felt that I needed to have a heart-to-heart talk with God. I decided to meet with my Heavenly Father at an historical site called Battle Rock State Park, which was on the outskirts of town. It was the site of a fierce Indian battle against white encroachment that had taken place during the time of the area's beginning settlements. The huge rock stood right on the beach of Oregon's beautiful rugged southern coast, which was littered with driftwood. I climbed up to the top of the rock and then proceeded down to the opposite side, so I could get away from the tourists. I didn't want to be seen by anyone except God. All alone on the rock, I poured out my heart to God and in my spirit, like Jacob of old, I wrestled with the Angel of the Lord. I petitioned my Heavenly Father, "What am I to do now that I am unemployed and have a burden for ministry?"

Feeling insecure, useless, and rejected of men, I wept. My Father God met me where and when I needed Him. He comforted me and reassured me of His divine love for me, speaking to my spirit, *"Wilt thou not from this time cry unto me, My father, thou art the guide of my youth?"* (Jeremiah 3:4).

Having lost my first father by death and my second father by divorce, I was left to consider my only true father to be my Heavenly Father. I always felt very close and special to Him who *"careth for me"* (I Peter 5:7).

In His still, small, and unmistakable voice, the Lord began to speak, "I am calling you unto Me for full-time service. You will never work for man again and receive a paycheck for services rendered. You are to trust Me, and I will provide for you and guide you."

It was marvelous! I felt refreshed and strengthened. Words can't explain what a tremendous transformation took place in my life. *I knew that I knew, that I knew*, that my Father God would somehow take care of me and provide for all my needs and those of my family.

I don't know how much time I spent embraced in the presence of God, but eventually I felt His presence leave. I got up from the rock with a new hope and courage to begin my ministry and serve God for the rest of my life. I would go anywhere He would lead and say anything He would command. I would never again look toward the world for provision—only to God. The year was 1979, and I was thirty-one years old.

With great excitement, I went home to tell Marilyn what the Lord had revealed to me on Battle Rock. After I shared with her all the words of the Lord, she simply said in her level-headed manner, "How are we going to provide for ourselves?"

Her question was of significance, and I didn't know the answer, so I said, "I'll have to go ask God and come back with an answer."

I left the kitchen where our conversation had taken place and went into the den. There, I knelt down beside the couch and asked, "Lord, how am I going to provide for our family since You gave me strict orders to never receive a paycheck for services rendered from an employer?"

Immediately, the Lord spoke to my spirit and said, "You're to serve and give your time to the people in your community without pay, and I will move upon their hearts to give as I direct."

Then the Lord reminded me of the word and message on "giving" that He had sent to me several years earlier through Pete, the elderly lady buying the socks from me at Henshey's Department Store. He then told me to read Isaiah 55 and share it with Marilyn, so I opened my Bible to the commanded Scripture. I couldn't believe how relevant the passage was to my prayer and question to the Lord.

> *"Ho, every one that thirsteth, come ye to the waters, and he that hath no money; come ye, buy, and eat; yea, come, buy wine and milk without money and without price. Wherefore do ye spend money for that which is not bread? and your labor for that which satisfieth not? hearken diligently unto me, and eat ye that which is good, and let your soul delight itself in fatness. Incline your ear, and come unto me: hear, and your soul shall live; and I will make an everlasting covenant with you, even the sure mercies of David"* (Isaiah 55:1-3).

I got up from my knees with an answer to my prayer and a word for Marilyn. She listened as I told her what the Lord had revealed to me and given me in Isaiah. In response, she simply said, "I don't understand with my intellect, but I will trust you, however the Lord leads you." Of my precious wife, Marilyn, I can truly say, *"Favour is deceitful, and beauty is vain: but a woman that feareth the LORD, she shall be praised"* (Proverbs 31:30).

CHAPTER 23

Where the Lord Guides, He Provides

I began to implement all that the Lord had instructed me to do in regard to serving my community. My role in the church was to work with the youth department. Particularly, I discipled Royal Rangers and youth from our community, which included both boys and girls. I devoted myself full-time to working with youth of all ages in after-school programs and during midweek, Friday, and Sunday church services. I spent many hours doing "Release Time" ministry on high school and elementary school grounds. (Release Time International is an organization that works with local city pastors throughout America to sponsor Bible training programs for public school students.) During my free time, I sought the Lord as to how I should go about providing for my family.

I want to share with you that learning to recognize the voice of the Lord is difficult and an issue that is of great controversy within the Body of Christ today. I don't intend for this book to be the grounds to justify what I believe as the Bible clearly defines the subject. You owe it to yourself to search God's Word on the matter. Suffice it for me to say, it is another one of those *I know that I know that I know* experiences. The truth of the doctrine that the Lord speaks to His people—His sheep (John 10)—is not null and void just because one does not know how to recognize the difference between the voice of the Lord and his or her own subconscious or the devil's voice of temptation. Therefore, I exhort you to search the Scriptures on the subject for your own benefit.

I remember learning how to recognize His voice. Sometimes, I learned the hard way, as in the time the Lord had instructed me to go visit a widow I had known from passing conversations. The Lord directed me to visit her and give her a bunch of wild flowers as a gesture of kindness. I had previously visited with her to encourage her in the Lord; however, I wasn't certain where she stood in regard to her salvation, so I was putting off the visit until I could determine the best way to share my faith with her.

On three separate occasions, as I drove by her home, which had a lovely and well-manicured rose garden, the Lord told me to visit her. I put it off and, to my regret, within one week of the Lord's prompting me to visit with her, she suddenly died. In my spirit and soul, I grieved. As I sought the Lord's forgiveness, I asked Him help me to never again to neglect His voice. I asked God to teach me to obey Him promptly.

Now, let me go back to telling you how the Lord provided for my family during the time I didn't have a job. While I was on one of my prayer walks (this has been my typical manner of prayer for over the past twenty-five years), the Lord prompted me to go up to a stranger's door and knock to ask if I could mow his lawn for him. I obeyed. When I knocked, an elderly lady answered.

"I notice that your lawn needs mowing," I said.

"I am a widow, and I don't have any money to pay you," she replied.

"You don't need to pay me. I'll gladly do it as a Christian act of servanthood."

She was overcome with surprise and consented to my labor of love. She was so nice that, from time to time, she came outside to thank me and offered me a glass of lemonade.

When I finished the job I knocked on her door and told her, "Good-bye." As I started to leave, she said, "I want to give you a donation for helping me." I tried to talk her out of doing so, but she insisted that I receive the money as "unto the Lord."

I left humbled and grateful to the Lord for leading me there and for His provision. God's provision was always exactly what was needed. God demonstrated His faithfulness and performed His Word as we learned, first hand, that *"...my God shall supply all your need according to His riches in glory by Christ Jesus"* (Philippians 4:19).

Another example of God's provision was when I needed leather to sew my buckskin Royal Ranger outfit for the Fellowship Camping Fraternity. We had a wonderful leather shop in town, which was run by a Christian couple, Mr. and Mrs. Walters. I often went to the shop to fellowship with the couple and, all the while, I would secretly drool over the leather wishing I could afford it. During one of my visits, Howard Walters told me that he needed to paint his building, which was a huge two-story structure. I asked him if I could paint it for him free of charge, but he said, "No."

I replied, "I don't work for pay but only to do the Lord's service."

Howard's comeback was, "You can work for a donation of money and leather."

"You've got a deal!" I was elated. Howard didn't know that I wanted leather to make my outfit, but the Lord did, and He was making provision!

I borrowed scaffolding and a paint sprayer from the local school district and began painting. About two weeks later, I completed the job and walked home happy as a lark because I had enough leather to make my *entire* buckskin outfit. For three months I hand stitched my outfit including all the Indian beadwork. Today, the outfit is worth $1,500. My buckskin outfit has been used as an evangelistic tool in numerous ways throughout the U.S.A. It has been used by God to lead countless numbers of children to Christ as I have woven the Gospel message with a mountain man or Indian theme story of one sort or another. Not having a job and pursuing my desire to follow Jesus left me with no choice but to live a life of faith. Living the life of faith can be scary and, at the same time, exhilarating. I wouldn't trade this lifestyle for "all the tea in China."

God granted us another remarkable answer to prayer in the area of provision. One Christmas season, Marilyn expressed to me in private that she longed for a roast beef for our Christmas meal. Now, this may seem strange to some, but for Marilyn it was perfectly normal as she is from Scottish descent. As turkeys are a part of the typical American tradition, so roast beef is typical of the British tradition.

As a husband, I wanted to please my wife and provide her every need and desire whenever possible. I contemplated her desire, but a roast was so much more expensive than a turkey. I was doubtful that I could buy a turkey, much less a roast. My faith was little in regard to such a request. In passing, I silently mentioned my wife's request to the Lord. *"Casting all your care upon Him; for*

He careth for you" (I Peter 5:7). I asked the Lord to lead me. I left my request at His feet and went about my merry way thinking, "A Christmas turkey would be blessing enough as there are many times when we don't have enough money even to know where our next carton of milk is going to come from."

Our faith may have wavered at times but the Lord always provided our needs and sometimes our desires too. What amazed me was that the Lord never provided in the same way twice. In His infinite wisdom and abundance, He always guided and provided in a unique way. During one of those times when we were wondering what our next meal would be, I came home and found outside our front door a bag of three freshly skinned chickens that the Lord had prompted someone to place there anonymously.

Christmas was fast approaching, and I had resigned to forgo getting anything but yams to eat for our Christmas meal. However, two days before Christmas, we heard a knock at the door. When we opened the door, we saw Mr. Leo Phillips, the father of our dear friend, Steve Phillips, the boat builder. Mr. Phillips said, "Merry Christmas, Wheelers! The Lord prompted my wife, Dodie, and me to bring over a Christmas turkey to thank you for your service in our church."

We were blessed and grateful beyond words. A big hug sufficed as we were too choked up to say much of anything else. Now, at least, we could add turkey to our Christmas dinner. The thought of having only yams for dinner hadn't seemed very appealing.

The next day, on Christmas Eve, we heard another knock at the door. This time, we found Steve Phillips, himself, standing out in the cold with a brown bag. As Steve stepped into our living room, he wasn't aware that his dad had been over the day before with a turkey, and we weren't about to tell him since we were in such dire need. Marilyn and I were both thinking that we could have the second turkey for our New Year's dinner, so I said, "Steve, thank you so very much. We love turkey. It's so good, and the leftovers make great enchiladas and tacos. Praise God!"

Steve said, "Wait a minute! Don't get your hopes up too high because, while I was about to pick up a turkey, Carol and I decided perhaps we should get you a ham."

By this time, my mind was reeling with excitement. I thought to myself, "We can have Mr. Phillips' turkey for Christmas and Steve's ham for New Year's dinner. We won't have to eat so much turkey and get sick of having turkey for both holidays."

Steve continued talking and then said, "We're really sorry, but for some strange reason we didn't feel that we should get you a traditional turkey or a ham. Instead, we got you a six-pound roast."

We had tried to conceal our tears from Mr. Phillips, Steve's dad, but now we were unable to hold back our tears of gratitude. In Steve's presence, our tears streamed forward as we experienced God's love and overwhelming assurance of His care and provision. We hadn't told a single person on the face of the earth about Marilyn's desire for a Christmas roast; yet, God knew and, in His love and mercy, He provided.

God has provided so many things for us over the years since then. However, next to our gift of salvation, the Christmas roast has been the greatest blessing that He has given us. That roast caused us to be encouraged and built up in our faith and knowledge of God, our Father, as our eternal Provider. I can't get over the fact that God heard our private conversation and responded without our having to toil in prayer about it. It was as if God especially cared for my wife and wanted to bless her.

> *"Therefore I say unto you, Take no thought for your life, what ye shall eat, or what ye shall drink; nor yet for your body, what ye shall put on. Is not the life more than meat, and the body than raiment? Behold the fowls of the air: for they sow not, neither do they reap, nor gather into barns; yet your heavenly Father feedeth them. Are ye not much better than they? ....Wherefore, if God so clothe the grass of the field, which today is, and tomorrow is cast into the oven, shall He not much more clothe you, O ye of little faith?   Therefore take no thought, saying, What shall we eat? or, What shall we drink? or, Wherewithal shall we be clothed? . . . for your heavenly Father knoweth that ye have need of all these things. But seek ye first the kingdom of God, and His righteousness; and all these things shall be added unto you" (Matthew 6:25-33).*

CHAPTER 24

Angel Eyes

Before we moved to Port Orford, Oregon, and while making plans to move away from Southern California, I had to face some of the most difficult decisions of my life. Leaving California meant that I had to say good-bye to my dearest friend and mentor, Earl Brent. At the time, Earl was battling cancer, and I would visit him often at the Santa Monica Hospital. He gave me his blessing to move, but he also told me that he didn't think that he could face another surgery. He said, "The next one will kill me."

I refused to accept what he said. "You *will* get well, and I will take you home to recuperate," I assured him. Side-by-side, his sister, Rosemary, and I took care of him. However, within a very short time, Earl died. I lost one of the greatest friends I would ever know. Over thirty years my senior, he was my Elijah. I have never forgotten him nor will I ever. The only comfort I received was that I knew Earl went to be present with the Lord and, one day, we would be reunited in Christ Jesus.

After Earl's death, Rosemary found his last will and testament. In his will, Earl had honored me by appointing me to be the executor of his estate. I knew it would take time to sift through everything, and we were going to be moving two weeks later, so I hired a lawyer.

True to his word, Earl Brent had left me as beneficiary to all the royalties of the songs he had composed over the years. At the time, I didn't quite know just what it all meant, but God was going to use those quarterly royalty checks in ways that I could never have dreamed possible. Whenever Earl's songs were played in a movie or sung by performers, such as Frank Sinatra, Jack Jones, Tony Bennett, and Willy Nelson, royalties were generated. One such song was "Angel Eyes" which was co-written with Matt Dennis. Every three months, the royalties were added up and distributed.

Providentially, about the time Steve, the boat builder, had discharged me and the Lord was calling me into His service full-time, Earl Brent's estate was settled. I'll never forget the time that we received our first royalty check. It was wonderful!

All my life I dreamed of owning my own washer and dryer. I was so poor growing up that my mom and I had to walk down to the Laundromat to do our laundry. I vividly remember how embarrassed I was as I toted our wire-frame basket home from the Laundromat. The whole world could see me with that basket filled with my clothes along with my mother's and sister's clothes! Being a young teen-aged boy, it was truly traumatic and humiliating. I really believed that only rich people could afford a washer and dryer.

After five years of marriage, Marilyn and I still didn't own such appliances, so guess what I decided to blow our first royalty check on? You're right—a harvest gold Whirlpool washer and dryer! Wow! After I finished installing our new appliances on the uneven floor of our dilapidated service porch, I stood for a long time just staring at them. Then I pushed and punched every button that I could find several times—just for the sheer joy of it! "Imagine washing and drying clothes without having to have quarters!" I said to myself.

Marilyn got a real kick out of watching me play with my new toys. My dream of twenty years had been fulfilled, as I *finally* owned my own washer and dryer.

CHAPTER 25

The Ministry

The church never was able to increase my salary. In fact, eventually, they had stopped supporting us altogether. In His infinite wisdom, God foresaw this and provided the royalty checks to carry us through. If we lived frugally, we could live off the amount provided by the royalty checks.

On my thirtieth birthday, November 24, 1978, the Assemblies of God gave me a license to preach. I was thrilled to receive my license at the same age that Jesus had begun His public ministry. Two years later, after taking the prescribed Bible training, I received my ordination. I continued to minister to young people, and I learned many important lessons regarding youth ministry.

When I began in full-time ministry, I was much too young and lacked experience to know what I now know. Generally speaking, I no longer subscribe to the para church ministry of having a "youth pastor" and "youth groups." Over the past eighteen years, I have witnessed more examples of disaster than success in youth ministry. Furthermore, there are no Biblical grounds for youth ministries to be governed by a "youth pastor." In fact, the Bible admonishes church leaders *not* to place a novice in a position of authority. The only "youth ministry" that I believe has any Biblical grounds is one that is governed by parents who are willing to take on the responsibility of discipling and ministering to their teens.

I became disheartened with what I saw in the

church. I was especially discouraged by the church's willingness to adapt to the clothing, manners, entertainment values, and general attitudes of unsaved youth and carnal Christians. It was like playing the game "Chutes and Ladders"; the young people would progress ten paces, only to backslide fifteen. The majority of youth that I discipled over the years were involved in drinking, drugs, chewing and smoking tobacco, fornication, unwholesome music, and ungodly videos. I saw no distinction between the church youth group and the rebellious unsaved youth. The only difference was that the church youth were trying to read their Bibles and live a Christian life. They were sitting on the fence and embracing both worlds. Sadly and amazingly, the parents knew nothing of the sin in which their teens were involved. The parents perceived their teenagers to be angels, and if they displayed any inappropriate behavior it was attributed to the diabolical psychological deception that "it's just part of being an adolescent."

Needless to say, I wanted to get out of youth ministry, and I wanted the parents to take responsibility for their own youth. Providentially, God opened a way for me to begin ministering in other capacities. The Royal Rangers were having me minister at powwows throughout the state of Oregon, and I gained recognition as an able communicator to elementary-aged children. Doors began to open for me to minister at Royal Rangers camps throughout the entire Pacific Northwest as my FCF name of "Little Bear" began to precede me.

One day, I decided to visit our local Assemblies of God district headquarters. I drove the five hours away from our home to see if they would allow me to minister at their state boys' and girls' summer camps. Outfitted in my mountain man buckskin outfit, I looked up the Assistant

Superintendent, Pastor Al Davis, and introduced myself. Pastor Al gazed at me over the top of his eyeglasses with suspicion. Evidently, he wasn't accustomed to seeing a man in his office dressed like Davy Crockett with a coon skin hat. He asked me, "Have you ever done any children's camps?"

"No," I answered. "But I have been working with children in my local church as well as with Child Evangelism Fellowship."

"That isn't good enough," he said. "I need someone who has experience with boys' and girls' camps."

My spirit was really hurt. It reminded me of my show business days. The producers and directors would always ask, "Do you have any experience?"

If I said "No," they wouldn't let me audition. I could never figure out how a person could get experience if he never even had a chance to try out.

Again, even though I was in full-time ministry, I was in the same old "Catch-22," this time it was in Christian terms. I walked out of the Oregon headquarters disillusioned and bewildered.

I'd been in full-time ministry for only about one year, and I could have become embittered by the experience. But thanks be to God, I have always had the type of personality that isn't bent toward resentfulness or vindictiveness.

As I placed my hand on the door to leave the building, the Lord spoke to me in a wonderful and gentle way saying, "I'll make it right someday." It wasn't until four years later that I discovered what the Lord had meant.

I turned my disappointment into "His appointment" by going to the Lord in prayer and seeking His comforting Word. During my appointment, the Spirit of the Lord led me to Revelation 3:7 *"And to the angel of the church in Philadelphia write; These things saith He that is holy, He that is true, He that hath the key of David, He that openeth, and no man shutteth; and shutteth, and no man openeth."*

The Spirit of the Lord was telling me that *He* would give me the keys to the Kingdom and that I didn't need for man to open the doors of opportunity for me to minister the Gospel.

The Lord then instructed Marilyn and me never to seek for opportunities to minister by soliciting through the mail or by telephone. In fact, we weren't to promote our ministry at all. It was clear that we were to wait on Him to open doors of opportunity. *"For promotion cometh neither from the east, nor from the west, nor from the south. But God is the judge: he putteth down one, and setteth up another"* (Psalm 75:6-7).

It was a difficult step of faith, but I was determined to apply my life verse to the situation. *"Trust in the Lord with all thine heart; and lean not unto thine own understanding. In all thy ways acknowledge Him, and He shall direct thy paths"* (Proverbs 3:5-6). The Lord was building the foundation upon which He intended our ministry to be based. I decided to seek counsel from our pastor regarding how to raise our financial support since it appeared that the Lord was leading us into an evangelical ministry. Pastor Mike was fairly new to the ministry himself and suggested that I write letters asking friends to support our ministry. He told me that from what he had seen in ministry, evangelists and missionaries needed to raise a support base. I returned home and shared his counsel with Marilyn. We didn't have a peace about using such means, but since we were new in ministry, we thought perhaps we should follow his advice. I regret not having prayed longer and getting the Lord's approval. Instead, I opened our family address book and began with the letter "A." With pen in hand, I composed a letter to two dear friends. The first letter was to a widow who had been a family friend and had known Marilyn as a child. The second letter was to a couple we knew. It didn't take very long to get back a response.

We received the widows letter first, and it read nearly like this:

Dear Richard and Marilyn,

I am very hurt that you have asked me to support you as I am on a fixed income. I can't even support myself and so my children supplement my monthly income. I would love to help out but I just can't and so your request has put me in a very awkward position. I am amazed that you would stoop so low as to ask a widow for money.

Sincerely,

Mrs. A_____

Her rebuke did the job. I felt so low and dirty that I wanted to crawl under the table and hide in shame. Mortified, I began to cry and repent of what I had done. *"The earth, O LORD, is full of thy mercy: teach me thy statutes . . . It is good for me that I have been afflicted; that I might learn thy statutes . . . I know, O LORD, that thy judgments are right, and that thou in faithfulness hast afflicted me"* (Psalm 119:64-75).

The final straw came the next day when we received a letter from the wife of the couple to whom I had written. Enclosed with the note was five dollars:

Dear Richard and Marilyn,

I am very happy to see that the Lord is calling you into full-time evangelistic ministry; however, I am very sorry that we will not be able to help you financially since Jack has had many unexpected medical expenses. I have enclosed five dollars to help you. I am sorry that I have not enclosed more of a gift, but it is all that I have at this time to give.

With much love,

The A_____

You can well imagine how miserable I felt. Marilyn had to bite her tongue to keep from saying, "I told you so."

But even a blind man could see how I looked and felt, so she just comforted me. I wrote back to both of our dear friends and thanked them for their letters and their loving rebuke that I so needed *"For whom the LORD loveth He chasteneth, and scourgeth every son whom He receiveth"* (Hebrews 12:6). Then I fell on my knees and told the Lord that I would never again ask for support from man. The Lord spoke to my heart saying, "If you will never solicit funds or require a fee for speaking, I will meet your needs more than sufficiently." *"For whom the LORD loveth He correcteth; even as a father the son in whom He delighteth"* (Proverbs 3:12).

By His Holy Spirit, God continued to teach me

other invaluable lessons that I have never forgotten. *"But the Comforter, which is the Holy Ghost, whom the Father will send in my name, He shall teach you all things . . ."* (John 14:26). The Lord revealed to me that ministries which seek the support of men will fail because they trust in the arm of the flesh—the arm of the flesh always fails. The Lord spoke to my heart, "If you will seek Me alone for provision, I will guide and provide. If money doesn't come in, it is like a well that goes dry—it is an indication to go and dig another well."

I began to see the pity of those ministries that sought money from man through bank loans, financial schemes, and their spoken appeals in order to build their empires. Many of them have failed and have come under judgment in my lifetime because they trusted in man rather than the Lord of all. I got up from the floor determined to walk by faith and to completely trust God for *everything*.

Another danger that the Lord revealed to me was that, if we campaigned money, our focus would be in the wrong place. Soliciting for money exemplifies a ministry's fear of man instead of the fear of God. In other words, we would be looking to man to supply our needs instead of God, and it would taint our ability to preach the truth with power. *"Teach me thy way, O LORD; I will walk in thy truth: unite my heart to fear thy name"* (Psalm 86:11).

Sadly, many churches become "seeker-friendly" in order to pay the debt on their buildings—*not* to reach the lost. The teachings that come from the Lord through prayer, sorrow, and repentance are so precious that I wouldn't trade them for the world. *"I will instruct thee and teach thee in the way which thou shalt go: I will guide thee with mine eye"* (Psalm 32:8).

Despite the rejection from Pastor Al Davis in

allowing me the opportunity to minister at children's camp, God was faithful to the Word He had given me. Just as God promised, He opened many doors of opportunity for me to minister.

Several years later, I ministered at a crusade for children in Lebanon, Oregon, with Pastor Garland Rodgers. On Wednesday night of the crusade, I had an altar call in which several young children gave their hearts and selfish wills to the Lord Jesus Christ.

After the Friday evening service of the crusade, the youth pastor came up to me to thank me for coming and for being used by God to show his seven-year-old son the way to the Savior, Jesus Christ. He went on to explain, "My wife and I have been waiting for the Lord to show our son the Savior as we didn't want to pressure him into being saved. We wanted to make sure that he became a Christian because he saw his need for the Savior and not because his mom and dad are Christians."

The youth pastor had been out of town the Wednesday night I had the altar call for the children. When he had called home that evening, after the service, his son had told him all about how he received Jesus Christ as his personal Savior.

Then the youth pastor said to me, "Have you ever considered doing children camps? You'd be great!"

I responded by telling him, "Four years ago, your father told me I wasn't good enough!"

You guessed it! The youth pastor was the son of Pastor Al Davis, the Assistant Superintendent for the Assemblies of God! The boy who received salvation was his very own grandson.

Then the Holy Spirit spoke to my heart and reminded me of the time, four years earlier, when I had left the state office as a reject in the eyes of Pastor Al Davis and God had told me, "I'll make it up to you someday." What an awesome God we serve!

During the years of transition from full-time youth pastoring to full-time evangelism, Marilyn and I were blessed to have another child by natural childbirth. It was a wonderful experience to be able to attend and to participate in my own child's birth. Aimee was born June 3, 1980, in Gold Beach, Oregon, where she arrived in a midwife's birthing home overlooking the beach.

A major turning point occurred in my ministry when I took our church youth group to a youth retreat at a camp in Southern Oregon. That year, the camp speaker was a former Vietnam soldier named Dave Roever. Dave has an incredible evangelistic ministry and is used by God in powerful ways.

After one of the meetings during that week, I had the opportunity to fellowship with Dave and obtain his counsel. I asked him, "How does a person know whether or not God is calling him into full-time evangelism?"

We talked for some time, and I will never forget what he said. "The gift of evangelism is a much-needed gift in the Body of Christ and a worthy calling, but I must warn you, as you progress in the labor of evangelism, don't give into the temptation of becoming a pastor. Sadly, many times, because the labor of evangelism is great, a man who is called to be an evangelist chooses instead to become a pastor."

I asked, "So, how am I going to become *known* when I am an *unknown*?"

He gave me a word that has, to date, been fulfilled to the letter. He answered, "You will find that as the Lord opens small doors of opportunity and you step through them, you will leave behind a circle of influence."

He then gave me a word picture of a pond. "Each time you speak somewhere, it is like throwing a small rock into a pond. Speaking at another meeting, in a different city, is like throwing another rock into the pond, only in a different place. After several years, the circle of water rings resulting from throwing the rocks in will begin to run together. At that point, you will have enough work and will be busy speaking all year."

Today, eighteen years later, we have been in forty-eight states and have ministered in every imaginable setting. I praise God and thank Dave Roever for taking time to counsel me during those early and fearful years of my first baby evangelist steps.

Before proceeding with more of my life story, I would like to share two events from our Port Orford days that the Lord used to help me grow in our ministry. I have discovered over the years that the best Bible school to attend is the "school of life."

The first event occurred after coming home from a three-month motor home tour. I received a telephone call from a total stranger. Giving no introduction whatsoever, the stranger said, "Are you ready for this weekend?"

Fumbling and stuttering, I tried to make my brain remember some previous conversation that I may have forgotten. I pretended to know what he was referring to and said, "Well—yes, I am ready. I always try to be ready when the Lord calls. Are you ready?"

He eagerly answered, "I'm ready, and I have my marriage license in proper order. Mike told me that you would do my wedding!"

I had never met the man or his bride. I cringe to think that I actually performed a couple of weddings in those early years of ministry without really knowing the couple or giving them proper counsel.

He then told me, "My name is Ira, and I plan to have the ceremony at "Mother's Rock."

I had no idea where, on that primitive rocky coast of Oregon, Mother's Rock was located. Puzzled, I asked, "Which Mother's Rock?"

In his carefree and cocky manner he insisted, "You know, Mother's Rock—about five miles off shore. I just got my twenty-foot fishing boat delivered. We can all get on board and take her out on her maiden voyage, get married, and do the whole thing at one time."

"What time do you plan on getting married?" I asked.

"Six o'clock in the morning."

I gasped.

Hearing my response, Ira said, "What's the matter? Is that too early for you?"

"Well, it certainly isn't too early for me being an old fisherman, but for the wedding party and your new bride, it might be too early."

We concluded our conversation by agreeing to show up at a more civil hour—9:00 a.m. Then, just before hanging up, Ira asked, "You got one of them preacher hats, don't ya?"

"Preacher hat?" I had no idea what he was talking about.

"You know," he insisted, "the kind Gary Cooper wears in them movies when he plays the part of a preacher."

It just so happened that, of all the citizens in our illustrious city of Port Orford, I was probably the only person to have such a hat. It was part of my Pilgrim outfit.

Later, I found out that Ira worked as a demolition expert setting up explosives to be used in various Hollywood movies. He was so ignorant of God that he figured a *real* preacher had to have a "preacher's hat" as he was accustomed to seeing on the sets.

On Saturday morning, we all showed up and I was introduced to the man who built Ira's boat. As I looked over the boat, I noticed there wasn't a single life jacket or survival suit for any one of us five soon-to-be passengers. If someone were to go overboard anywhere along the southern coast of Oregon, he or she would have roughly five minutes before hypothermia set in and the person would be sent straight down to "Davy Jones's locker." Besides having no survival suits, there wasn't a communications radio either, which meant there was no way of calling someone in the case of an emergency.

I became even more concerned when Ira told the dock crew, as they lowered the brand new boat into the water, "Come rescue us at Mother's Rock if we aren't back in two hours."

I wanted to back out of my commitment, but it was too late. I was already aboard and heading out into the water. The boat engine was fired up, and off we sped into the deep blue yonder. As we approached Mother's Rock, I could see its beauty. It was a huge mass of rocks jutting out of the water, and it was covered with seals. Some of the seals were sleeping while others were playing and frolicking together or diving into the ice-cold Pacific.

Ira was such a unique and impulsive individual that, as we were cruising around looking for just the right spot to perform the wedding ceremony, he shouted to the skipper, "Stop the boat right here!"

We came to a screeching halt, and Ira grabbed a deep-sea fishing rod and cast it out. Within three minutes he had caught a red snapper. He called out to his soon-to-be wife, "Barb, honey, come on over here and reel in the first fish you've ever caught."

Barb smiled as if to say, "Yes, dear. This really isn't the time to stop and fish. *But*, if *you* want me to make you happy by reeling in *'your'* fish, then I'll do it—even though I *am* in *my* wedding dress."

She reeled in the fish, up and over the rail of the boat. Ira was so ecstatic that he proclaimed it to be a "Kodak moment." He bellowed saying, "This is a momentous occasion and worthy of a picture."

At this point, a camera appeared and Barbara was made to hold up the seven-pound red snapper with its eyes bulging out of its sockets while Ira instructed her to say, "Smile!" She did and Ira slapped her on the back and congratulated her on her big catch. Then he commanded the skipper to move the boat to an appropriate location for the wedding ceremony.

Moments later, Ira yelled, "Stop! This is it!"

He then looked at me and said, "Do it!"

I took this as my cue to stand up and get ready for the ceremony. I put on my tall black "preacher's hat" and moved in front of Ira and Barbara, who had their backs to the bow of the boat. I administered the typical traditional marriage ceremony. In the closing statement, I addressed Ira saying, "Repeat after me: In the name of the Father, the Son, and the Holy Spirit, Amen!"

Ira repeated, "In the name of the Father, the Son—and who's that other guy?"

I said, "The Holy Spirit."

"And the Holy Spirit," he repeated with a puzzled look on his face. Barbara did much better at her vows and had more of an understanding of what marriage was all about.

As time passed on while living in Port Orford, I grew to love this couple and I pray that they have remained faithful to each other over the years. However, I shudder when I think of my inexperience and the many mistakes I made in those days. I certainly wouldn't call a young man into church ministry without providing him with the direct supervision of a senior pastor. An Elisha needs an Elijah.

We must be wise and take heed to the instructions given in I Timothy 3:1-6:

> *"This is a true saying, If a man desireth the office of a bishop, he desireth a good work. A bishop then must be blameless, the husband of one wife, vigilant, sober, of good behaviour, given to hospitality, apt to teach; Not given to wine, no striker, not greedy of filthy lucre; but patient, not a brawler, not covetous; One that ruleth well his own house, having his children in subjection with all gravity; (For if a man know not how to rule his own house, how shall he take care of the church of God?) Not a novice, lest being lifted up with pride he fall into the condemnation of the devil. Moreover he must have a good report of them which are without; lest he fall into reproach and the snare of the devil."*

I am eternally grateful to the Lord that He used me in spiritual matters, in spite of my ignorance, and continues to use me. My greatest desire and prayer is to be an asset to the Lord and a joy to Him in my behavior. May He continue to be patient with me, teach me, and guide me in spite of my mistakes. *"Keep back thy servant also from presumptuous sins; let them not have dominion over me: then shall I be upright, and I shall be innocent from the great transgression. Let the words of my mouth, and the meditation of my heart, be acceptable in thy sight, O LORD, my strength, and my redeemer"* (Psalm 19:13-14).

Another event occurred during our early years of ministry that had a significant bearing on the future course of my life. Obviously, living in the primitive southern coastal region of Oregon afforded to me wonderful opportunities to hunt, trap, and practice my pioneering skills. I was able to shoot my black powder rifle, throw tomahawks and knives, practice my quick draw and trick shooting, and go hunting. Hunting always occurred during the middle of October when the weather was beautiful and God was displaying His glory in the changing colors of the foliage. I loved being able to enjoy God's handiwork and was thankful for this beautiful time of the year. I also enjoyed the opportunity to get away from the city and go up into the mountains where I could be with my Heavenly Father in solitude and commune with Him in prayer. Marilyn has always understood and has been very good to me in regard to this need in my life.

One year while I was deer hunting within an hour's drive from town, the Lord spoke to my spirit and said, "Do you enjoy hunting?"

I said, "Oh, yes, Lord—you know how much I love to be up here with You and Your creation."

He then asked, "If I gave you more opportunities to minister during the month of October, which would you choose to do—hunt or minister?"

I was so amazed. It was as if the Lord was really giving me a choice. Up until that day, I always thought that humans were simply dumb creatures who had to respond and do whatever the Lord bids them to do. Ultimately, I figured that we didn't have any choice in the matter, so I was surprised when the Lord seemingly gave me a choice.

Since I depended strictly upon the Lord to book my meetings, I had to wait for Him to open the doors of opportunity to speak at churches, camps, schools, conventions, and conferences. Notably, the month of October always had plenty of free time left on the calendar, so I naturally took that time to hunt. Now, the Lord was giving me a chance to choose between hunting or ministry. I felt as though my Heavenly Father was considering my will and desire over His own. I thought to myself, "I must really be growing up since my Father is allowing me to make a choice on my own!"

To be completely honest, it was a difficult choice. I was able to hunt deer only three weeks out of the year, and my ministry potential was eleven months. As I walked down an old logging road, I contemplated the question for a considerable time. Then I answered, "Lord, if You're giving me the choice and leaving it up to me, then I believe it would be more expedient, providing You open the doors, for me to minister than for me to hunt. I'll gladly give up hunting. After all, I can pray to You anytime and anywhere. I don't have to be here in the mountains to pray."

Immediately, the Lord spoke to my heart saying, "You've made a wise choice—the one I was hoping you would make. And because of your choice, I will give you so many opportunities to minister in the month of October that you won't be able to find time to hunt. Instead, I will give you souls to hunt. It is always open season for the salvation of My people."

I put away my rifle, and by the next deer season, true to His word, the Lord had booked so many meetings for me that deer hunting was a thing of the past. That particular decision marked a major growth and change in my life. I remembered, once before, that I had to choose between Marilyn and skinning a prized gray squirrel; this time I had to choose between my love for the outdoors and ministering to a greater measure for the Lord. I died to self so that I could live more abundantly in Christ. Isn't this what life is all about? *"He must increase, but I must decrease"* (John 3:30). *"All things are lawful unto me, but all things are not expedient: all things are lawful for me, but I will not be brought under the power of any"* (I Corinthians 6:12).

CHAPTER 26

A Message Is Born

Over the years, many people have asked me how I get the messages that I preach and teach. Oftentimes, I receive them during my prayer time or from just reading the Bible. At other times, I receive an inspiration by listening to my own pastor or to radio preachers. But my favorite messages come from my own life experiences and things that the Lord has taught me. After receiving an inspiration, I generally find an historical story that will carry the truth of the message home to the heart and intertwine it with the Word of God. One message that was born out of a personal experience and a lesson that the Lord taught me follows.

Back in the summer of 1980, I was conducting a series of meetings over a period of a few days at the Cody Assembly of God church in Cody, Wyoming. At the conclusion of one of our meetings, a young lady walked up to me and said, "I want you to have these couple of old coins that I have been saving for quite a while as a token of my appreciation."

She handed me a shields two-cent piece dated 1865 and an uncirculated 1885 silver dollar. The gift of coins was a pleasant surprise gift and brought back fond memories to me. As a young boy I took a fancy to collecting old pennies, nickels, dimes, and quarters in an amateur sort of fashion. Today, I think that it would be frustrating for a young lad or lass to collect coins, because all of the coins that have any value were taken out of circulation long ago. Rare coins were circulated among the general public when I was a child. Being young and lacking vision, I sold off my small-time collection. My old coins would be worth a pretty penny today (pardon the pun). As a result of the lady's giving me the two coins, I again was inspired to put together a coin collection from the 1800s time period. Therefore, I bought a special book to display the coins that were given to me. The book had slots in it so I could add to my collection.

As I saved a few extra dollars over the next couple of years, I invested in a coin or two to add to my unusual and rare coin collection. I always got a charge out of showing my two special coins to young people who had never seen or heard of a two-cent piece or a silver dollar. They would respond with remarks like "ooh" and "cool, man." I remember that whenever I went shopping with my book for a new coin, experienced coin dealers always spotted my special silver dollar out of the twenty or so coins I had collected. They would make comments like, "Let me see that a little bit closer" or "That silver dollar coin ought to be in a safe—not in a book like this." I always made light of their interest, but I realized that the coin was well worth over $250.

About two years after I had started collecting coins, I had saved enough money to add to my investment. I found myself shopping for my new coins in an Oregon coin shop. The dealer had taken a special interest in helping me find some potential coins to purchase. I gave him my book so he could help me look through his glass cases for coins that I needed to fill in the blank spots. I ended up purchasing two coins and walked out.

I held some meetings at a boys' and girls' camp in central Oregon about one month later. As I was ministering in my gold digger outfit, I decided to go to my props trailer and pull out my rare coin collection to show the elementary children. As I was thumbing through my coin book and got to the last page where I kept the old rare silver dollar, I discovered it was missing! It was gone! I panicked. I retraced in my mind, trying to recall who I had last allowed to hold my book, as I never let the book out of my sight when in a crowd or whenever someone looked through it. At first, I just couldn't figure out how the most valuable coin in my book could have been stolen.

Then, all of a sudden—like a flash of lightning—it dawned on me who the last person who had actually held my book. It was the coin dealer! I recalled that he had walked a slight distance from me when I wasn't paying close attention and was looking over my potential buying prospects. I was sick, angry, and to put it mildly — FUMING MAD! "How dare a dealer steal from a fellow coin collector," I thought to myself. I began to think evil thoughts like, "I hope that dealer goes out of business or that the police will catch him committing a crime and that he'll go to jail for life." By the time I had stewed over my plight for about two weeks, I had the dealer pretty much assigned to janitorial duty in the place of hell fire and brimstone.

Oh, you laugh—do you? Well, you ought not. You, too, have probably had someone who wronged you in your past. Just think back to all of the wicked things you thought about the person who wronged you. We are all made of the same sinful nature. It could just as easily be one of us who did someone wrong. The only difference is that, as Christians, we walk by the grace of God and can call upon His Holy Spirit to resist such a temptation and ask God to enable us to love our neighbor as ourselves (Matthew 22:39).

Whenever I remembered my experience with the coin dealer, I castigated him into the eternal regions of outer darkness. Believe me when I tell you that the memory came to my mind much too often due to the demons of hate, revenge, ill will, and my own flesh. Those demons of wickedness would not let the unjust deed pass from the archives of my mind until one day as I was driving east on Lombard Boulevard in Portland, Oregon, Jesus spoke to my spirit. I vividly recall that the word came so swiftly, without any immediate premeditation on my part, that it arrested my attention. The Lord said, "I took care of everything."

I responded, "You took care of what, Lord?"

"The coin dealer who stole your coin is going to hell just as you wanted," He replied.

I was shocked and said, "You mean just on *my* word alone that You are going to allow that man to go to hell?"

On that day, the Lord revealed some very profound truths to me that I will never forget. He instructed me that He has given believers power to "*bind and to loose*" (Matthew 16:19), and that if I chose to exercise this authority and condemn the coin dealer to hell then He would honor it. Whether or not the Lord was serious did not matter, as the idea itself caused me to become very concerned. I told the Lord, "I do not want to carry the responsibility of that man's soul upon my shoulders. No amount of money, stolen or not, in the world should or would warrant my sending a soul to hell."

"What do you propose I do then?" the Lord asked.

I considered the situation for a moment and then I realized that there was no alternative but for me to forgive the coin dealer and release him from his debt. So, I told the Lord, "I forgive the coin dealer of all sin against me, and I release him from defrauding me of my coin."

I immediately felt a spirit of peace flood my soul, and the anger that I was harboring for over a month was gone. It was wonderful! On the following day the Lord began to give me more instructions regarding forgiveness. He said, "It's a good thing that you forgave the coin dealer, because forasmuch as you have forgiven him, I will forgive you. Furthermore, inasmuch as you would *not* forgive him, I will *not* forgive you."

Then the Lord's Prayer was brought to my mind and the passage that says, *"And forgive us our debts, as we forgive our debtors"* (Matthew 6:12). The Lord also brought to my mind the parable of the king who forgave his servant a huge debt and, yet, that same servant who was forgiven so much would not forgive his fellow-servant who, in comparison, owed him a minuscule debt (Matthew 18:23-35).

I asked, "Lord, if I hadn't forgiven the coin dealer—would I have placed my soul in jeopardy of not receiving Your forgiveness when I stumble into sin?"

The Lord impressed upon me that it would certainly be the case. He revealed to me the awesome danger of unforgiveness—Satan cannot touch a blood-bought believer, but he can get a believer to curse himself through unforgiveness toward others. It was then that I could see the wicked ploy of the devil to use bitterness and an unforgiving spirit to cause a believer to self-destruct.

To further illustrate this truth, the Lord opened my understanding so that I could comprehend more amazing truths on the subject of forgiveness. He reminded me of two passages in the Bible demonstrating the power of forgiveness.

The first account on forgiveness is in the passage of Acts 7:58-60. When Stephen was being stoned to death by the Jewish Council in the city of Jerusalem, he cried out with a loud voice his final words saying, *"Lord, lay not this sin to their charge."* Then he fell asleep. Stephen could have called upon the Lord to judge his accusers for having a mock trial and would have been justified in doing so, but he chose to demonstrate the love of Christ instead. With this passage the Lord impressed a thought upon me that I will never forget. He said, "If Stephen had not spoken words of forgiveness as he breathed his last breath, Saul of Tarsus would not have become Paul the Apostle." Forgiveness allowed the Spirit of God eventually to bring Saul to Christ.

The second awesome account that the Lord illuminated for me on the subject of forgiveness is in Luke 23:32-34. When Jesus was crucified, He cried out, *"Father, forgive them; for they know not what they do."* The teaching that the Lord gave me on this passage was life changing. I had always wondered why the devil was so stupid as to demonically inspire the gathering crowd at the trial of Christ to ask for the death penalty. Surely Satan knew that the cross would result in his own defeat. So why would he seal his own doom by laboring and manipulating the people to get Jesus Christ to the cross? Things just did not make sense in my mind. However, the coin episode caused my lack of understanding to change. The revelation that came to me was that Satan, in his mind, had banked on the fact that what he had planned for the course of the crucifixion would bring total destruction to the entire human race. Now, the concluding scenario in the passage was making perfect sense to me.

Just a few days prior to the last Passover, Satan spoke through Peter in an effort to persuade Jesus not to go to Jerusalem because he feared that the cross would defeat him (Matthew 16:21-22). Christ responded by rebuking Peter and said, *"....Get thee behind me, Satan: thou art an offence unto me: for thou savourest not the things that be of God, but those that be of men"* (Matthew 16:23). At this point, it became apparent to Satan that Christ had gained the victory over the power of darkness through prayer in the Garden of Gethsemane because He submitted to His Father's will by saying, *"....O my Father, if it be possible, let this cup pass from me: nevertheless not as I will, but as thou wilt"* (Matthew 26:36-39). Submitting to God's will instead of our own will always make us the victor, *"Submit yourselves therefore to God. Resist the devil, and he will flee from you . . . Humble yourselves in the sight of the Lord, and He shall lift you up"* (James 4:7-10). As a result of Jesus' gaining the victory, Satan *had* to change his strategy.

I believe Satan chose the next evil ploy, which was to plan an attack of personal injury against the Son of God. Satan threw every dart of torture imaginable at the Lamb of God. Jesus was whipped to a pulp, beaten to smithereens, and mentally tortured beyond human comprehension. In His then physically and emotionally weakened condition, Christ had to carry the burden of the heavy cross. He suffered humiliation as He was stripped naked and lifted up in a torturous manner to hang before men, women, and children who jeered, taunted, and mocked Him incessantly. All the while, the Lamb of God was steadily losing His precious life-giving blood. I believe that Satan was hoping the whole time that, after being placed on the cross in this manner, Christ would lose His temper and become angry. Satan was certain that, rather than continuing to seek forgiveness for His tormentors, Jesus would curse the people and, by doing so, He would seal their eternal doom and that of the entire human race. I find it truly amazing that God was willing to forgive under such circumstances.

Think about it! Just recall the last time that you were feeling your very worst. Did you not want to just be left alone to suffer? Was not the pain so great that you had no patience left to be nice to people? Did you find yourself perhaps even hurting those you loved most even though that may not have been your intention? Conversely, can you imagine not hurting those who are your enemies? Having brought that to your mind, now multiply it a thousand times and you will begin to get a small glimmer of what Jesus Christ went through as a human—*not* as God Almighty.

Satan could not fathom that Christ would choose to forgive His tormentors. Keep in mind that if Jesus had blown it *just once* and become angry as Moses did when he hit the rock twice, it would have meant eternal damnation for all of mankind! Satan may have figured that, since Moses who was a "type of Christ" lost his cool and forfeited going into the Promised Land which was a type of Heaven, perhaps Christ would also lose His control, giving vent to His anger and also forfeit entering into the "Promise Land." If Satan had been right, he would have jumped with glee because mankind would have been lost in sin forever. But he was wrong! Jesus chose death to gain life and took the keys of hell and set the captives free! *"Whosoever shall seek to save his life shall lose it; and whosoever shall lose his life shall preserve it"* (Luke 17:33).

When Jesus Christ forgave His tormentors, He forgave us too. The Spirit of forgiveness at the cross paved the entrance into Heaven for all who seek the pardon of God through Christ Jesus. In other words, there is no sin that Jesus Christ cannot or will not forgive—except for the sin of rejecting Him and His precious blood that pardons. If God chose to forgive us, then why shouldn't we choose to forgive those who have hurt us?

CHAPTER 27

The Neighbor's Dog

Whenever the Lord teaches us a principle you can rest assured that He is also going to give us a test to see if we have truly learned the lesson. He wants the lesson to be in our hearts and our actions— not just be "head knowledge." The lessons are repeated much like the lesson the disciples learned when they requested that Jesus *"send the multitude away, that they may go into the villages, and buy themselves victuals"* (Matthew 14:15-21). Jesus told them that *"they need not depart,"* and then He performed the miracle that fed the people, and there still *"remained twelve baskets full."* Perhaps the Lord left one basket with food for each disciple as a reminder of God's provision.

Very little time had passed before the disciples found themselves in the same predicament. Once again, they approached Christ in a panic wondering what in the world they were going to do with such a large crowd and how they were going to feed them (Matthew 15:29-38). Surely, Jesus wondered why the disciples had not already learned the lesson that He had previously taught them. However, He was patient, loving, and kind enough to take what was available and increase it so *"they did all eat, and were filled."* Again Jesus made provision, but this time there *"was left seven baskets full."*

My test on the lesson of forgiveness came about one month after I had completely forgiven the coin dealer. I came home one dark and gloomy night and walked across my front lawn up to the porch. By this time I noticed a peculiar smell. It was coming from my shoes. I looked down and immediately identified the problem. You guessed it—my neighbor from two doors down had the nerve to allow his Springer Spaniel to mess on *my* grass!

I was fit to be tied. I hate mess on my shoes! My children had always begged me to get a dog but I wouldn't allow them to have one. I had always given them the "mess and shoe excuse" for not owning a dog. But there I was—not even owning a dog, and I had the "mess and shoe" problem! So I started my detective work and began staking out the neighbor's dog and its daily habits.

It didn't take long for me to notice that the dog made it a daily habit to use *my* yard for its "doggy duty." I became so angry that I couldn't stand it any longer. I determined to find a way to somehow punish the dog,—without anyone's knowing it of course. I thought, I schemed, and I plotted various dastardly punishments. However, each plan fell short of having an alibi, which I desperately needed so that even Sherlock Holmes wouldn't detect me. After all, what would people say if they knew the neighborhood evangelist hurt his neighbor's pet?

Finally, I came up with a seemingly good scheme that I was sure would work. The best part about my plan was that I thought I could do it without a single soul's ever knowing. I only needed to wait for just the right moment to execute my vengeance. One morning while I was planning the untimely death of my neighbor's dog, the Lord knocked on my heart and said, "Richard, may I talk to you for a moment?"

It was amazing, but I *knew* that the Lord wanted to talk to me about my dog plans. I was so convinced that I was justified in my deed that I actually had the audacity to answer the Lord by saying, "Yes—Lord, do *You* have a better way of punishing this pesky varmint?"

The Lord answered, "Yes!"

At this point I was all ears because I knew His ways were *always* better than mine. I could always count on God to work on getting rid of my problem. However, I was not quite prepared for the following words that pierced my spirit.

"Forgive the thoughtless owner of this dog," the Lord replied. "Do you really think that you will ever have a chance to share your faith with your neighbor if he finds out that you hurt his dog? Believe me when I tell you that he *will* find out. Besides, My Word says to *'be sure your sin will find you out'* (Numbers 32:23) and that your foolishness and sins are not hidden from Me (Psalm 69:5)."

Those words hit me like a bomb and exploded within my soul and spirit. I knew that the Lord was right and that I had no other recourse but to do what was right and forgive my neighbor and surrender my wicked ploy. I told the Lord, "You are right." Then I forgave my neighbor and his dog with the same attitude that I had for the coin dealer. The spirit of animosity that infected my soul left immediately. I was free to love my neighbor and his dog with the love of Christ. Love conquers all and covers a multitude of sins—even "dog duty."

The following morning when I looked out my breakfast nook window I spotted the dog mess in its usual place. However, this time I was happy to see the mess in my yard because I had been relieved of the burden of hate and I had the wonderful feeling of forgiveness. Love had flooded my soul. *"...Thou shalt love thy neighbour as thyself. Love worketh no ill to his neighbour...."* (Romans

13:9-10). So I joyously marched outside with my super-duper pooper-scooper in hand. I decided to use my time to pray for my neighbor's salvation while cleaning up the dog mess. Each day for about three days, I picked up the dog mess and prayed for the owner the whole time. It was wonderful to have a daily reminder and excuse to remember to pray for my neighbor.

Can you believe what happened? No— my neighbor didn't get saved as far as I know. But the dog stopped doing his business in my yard from that day forward. I figured the demons didn't like my praying for my neighbor's salvation, so they arranged for the dog to pick on someone else.

CHAPTER 28

Forgiveness Turned Silver into Gold

I thank God that, to this day, I do not have problems with letting things pass by that are offenses to me. In fact, the idea is so foreign to me now that I am surprised when I meet a Christian who carries a grudge. Some Christians carry them for a lifetime. I feel so sorry for them, and I wonder how they can live in the fullness of Christ while carrying the weight of unforgiveness. Before ending my testimony on the episode of the silver coin and forgiveness, I would like to tell you how good and faithful my Lord is to those who keep His commandments and do His will.

"But be ye doers of the word, and not hearers only, deceiving [cheating] *your ownselves. . . .But whoso looketh into the perfect law of liberty, and continueth therein, he being not a forgetful hearer, but a doer of the work, this man shall be blessed in his deed"* (James 1:22-25). The Lord shows *"mercy unto thousands of them that love"* Him and keep His commandments (Deuteronomy 5:10). Once we accept Jesus Christ as our Lord and Savior, it becomes much easier for us to obey God because we have been born again in our spirits. Our old nature from our carnal birth becomes subjective to His Spirit, as we are new creatures and old things have passed away (II Corinthians 5:17). We have His Spirit as we have been adopted into His family and have become His children. As children, we are obedient because we love our Heavenly

Father and we *want* to please Him. *"If ye love me, keep my commandments"* (John 14:15).

About two years after I had learned these valuable lessons on forgiveness, my family and I were leading some meetings in Southern California. One of the meetings was held at the home of a homeschool support group leader in Simi Valley. Bob and Kathy Likes had invited me to address their core group of leaders. After delivering the message the Lord had given me, Bob suggested that the group take up a kitchen pot offering as a love gift for Marilyn and me. The pot was given to me after the collection, so I decided to ask the Likes' twelve-year-old son to take the small offering and arrange the bills so they would all be facing in the same direction. After about ten minutes, their son came back up to me and said, "Little Bear, what is this?"

I looked down and noticed that he was holding a one-ounce gold coin. "Where did you get that?" I asked.

Bob Likes, who was standing next to me at the time, said, "I can't imagine who in our humble group would give such a valuable gift. That gold coin is worth about three hundred dollars!"

I was very much surprised at receiving such a gift. I carefully put it in my pocket and continued to fellowship with the families at the meeting.

Early the next morning during my habitual devotion and prayer time, the Lord spoke to my heart and said, "Inasmuch as you have learned to forgive the coin dealer who stole your silver coin, I have replaced it with a gold coin."

Wow! That is just like the Lord. Whatever we give to the Lord in life, it never returns to us void. To this day, I still carry that coin around and share the testimony of the forgiveness story. I want others to learn that, when we die to the wicked deeds of the flesh that are likened to the cheap dross of silver, the Lord rewards us with the purity of fine gold. The Lord desires that we be tried in order to bring up the dross so that we will become pure gold. Sometimes, it is only under great pressure and heat that hidden sins and false doctrine are brought to our attention. This produces an opportunity for us to acknowledge and confess our sins. It is at this point that our faithful God forgives us and cleanses us from all unrighteousness (I John 1:9). Therefore, we must *"count it all joy"* when we walk through the fiery trials of life (James 1:2). We ought to receive trials with eagerness as they prepare us to be the spotless and blameless Bride who is awaiting the return of her Groom—Jesus Christ. After all, He has promised her that she will reign with Him in His eternal Kingdom.

"I counsel thee to buy of me gold tried in the fire, that thou mayest be rich; and white raiment, that thou mayest be clothed, and that the shame of thy nakedness do not appear; and anoint thine eyes with eye-salve, that thou mayest see" (Revelation 3:18).

CHAPTER 29

A Big Step of Faith

As our ministry grew, I soon discovered that the Lord had used the previous twenty years to prepare and teach me the skills that were perfect for my calling. I was able to use quick draw, rope tricks, flint and steel fire starting and numerous other skills for the glory of God. While in costume I used my skills and props to relate historical messages, all in unison with the Word of God. The children loved it! I was amazed to see how the Lord had given me *"favor with God and man"* (Luke 2:52). I was beginning to get so many bookings throughout the year that I had to buy a small GMC van so I could tow a small utility trailer behind it for my props and costumes. My costumes were effective for presenting the Gospel in a very unique way: Pilgrim, Indian, gunfighter, cowboy, Civil War soldier, 1776 minuteman, and a variety of others.

Marilyn, Noelle, Aimee, and I soon outgrew the van, so we graduated to a seventeen-foot recreational vehicle. Two years later, we found our living quarters were, again, too small, so we purchased a twenty-four foot 1978 Country Camper with bunk beds. I make all this sound so simple and easy, but it was all accomplished by staying on our knees and petitioning the Lord to guide and provide for us, which He was always faithful to do. This was especially true since we had zero savings and were sustained only by receiving love gifts.

It soon became apparent that continuing to base our

ministry from Port Orford wasn't going to be very practical, because it took at least three hours to get out of town and onto a major highway. We felt as if we were never going to get to our destination. We sought the Lord for direction, and He answered us in a wonderful way.

While speaking at a Royal Rangers' powwow, which was one and a half hours away, just west of Portland, Oregon, I met a nine-year-old boy named Nathan Mendenhall. He gravitated toward me as if he were my own son. Through Nathan, I met his family. Within a very short period of time, our entire family became endeared to the hearts of this Christian family.

When the time came for us to move from Port Orford, we decided that our destination would be Portland, Oregon. We were blessed to have the Mendenhall family as our anchor. It was a practical move, because our ministry could conveniently travel in all directions while using Portland as a hub since the Pacific Northwest was the range of our growing ministry.

The only obstacle that stood in the way of our moving was the ability to sell our house, or should I say "shack," since Port Orford was generally financially depressed. But praise God, for if we follow and rest in Him, "His yoke is easy and His burden is light" (Matthew 12:30). I prayed about selling our house knowing that *"with God all things are possible"* (Matthew 19:26). We had fixed up our home the best we could with any extra money we could spare. Being a former roofer, I put on a new roof, which made the place look really cute despite the rotted window frames. White paint covered a multitude of "sins" such as dry rot and helped keep the windows intact.

I had learned to move in the direction of faith by trusting God to make the way, so I acquired some boxes from the local Sentry Market and told everyone we were moving. Bob the store manager, responded to me by saying, *"Sure* you're moving—fat chance you'll sell your home. Our house was on the market for two years with not so much as a nibble, and it's a much nicer home than yours."

I just smiled and said, "I am confident that God is requiring us to move to Portland to expand our ministry, and He will take care of it."

I took the boxes home and we packed up all of our things. We hand-painted a sign for the front yard that read "For Sale By Owner–$21,000–Inquire Within." Then we sat on the packed boxes and waited for the Lord to send us a buyer.

In a town of only 1,000 people, it doesn't take too long before everybody and their brother know that you're selling your place. So if you don't get a nibble or a bite within a month, you may as well be "tough luck Charlie" just as Bob had said at the Sentry Market. It is often humbling to walk by faith. Some people just snicker and poke fun at you with jokes like "Where is the promise of God?"

Actually, we were beginning to wonder ourselves if the Lord was going to sell our home. We questioned whether or not we should unpack. *"....O [we] of little faith, wherefore didst [we] doubt?"* (Matthew 14:31).

One day, as I was doing some touch-ups around the house, our Royal Ranger commander and friend, Gary Doran, came by to visit. I asked him, "How was the trip you took to California last month?"

After we had exchanged some small talk, he noticed the "For Sale" sign in our yard and said, "I didn't know you were contemplating selling your house."

I told him about my vision for moving to Portland, and he, in turn, told me that he was looking into investing in some rental property. The upshot of the story was that within one week of Gary's return from his trip, he and his wife bought our home! What was amazing to us was that when the Lord had prompted us to pack up our possessions, He already knew who was going to purchase our home! We didn't know who God had in mind and, from all outward indications, things looked hopeless. But that is exactly what faith is, *"Now faith is the substance of things hoped for, the evidence of things not seen"* (Hebrews 11:1). God was just beginning to do some mighty works on our behalf.

We moved our packed belongings into a storage unit in Portland, and then we moved our motor home into Al and Sherrie Mendenhall's backyard while we went house hunting. We had used a big chunk of the money from the sale of our home to pay off our motor home so that we wouldn't be burdened with debt. After the financial dust had settled, we had $7,000 cash in our hand. We suffered from shock when we began to look for a modestly priced home and saw how expensive they were.

I soon realized that $7,000 wasn't going to buy even a garage! So I proceeded to the bank to consult with a loan officer about securing a house loan. I was fairly ignorant in regards to securing a bank loan, but I went ahead anyway and filled out the necessary application form and submitted it to the loan officer. The first thing he asked me was, "What is your occupation?"

Of course I answered, "I'm an evangelist."

"What is an evangelist?" he questioned.

Right then and there, I knew I was headed for trouble because I figured that the next question would be, "How much money do you make?"

I was right! I explained to him, "Well, that depends on the size of the offerings. Sometimes it's enough to fill a hat, and other times it's enough to fill up my gas tank." Shaking his head, he said, "I'm sorry Mr. Wheeler, but we can't loan you any money because you are considered to be a high risk. Come back and see me when you have a secure job with a steady income."

I left the bank undaunted, because I had expected such a reply. After all, what does a loan officer know about the walk of faith? He didn't know that I was a son of the Father who owns the *"cattle upon a thousand hills"* (Psalm 50:10) and all the gold and oil besides. I turned to God in prayer and He assured me, "I will guide you to a house where the owner will carry the contract."

"Yes–of course!" I thought to myself.

Within a day or two, Marilyn and I spotted a jewel-of-a-house at 7114 North Chase, which was on the safe side of North Portland. We made arrangements to see it, and we both fell in love with it immediately. It was a *real* house with lots of rooms and *real* doorknobs! Compared to our Port Orford house, you would have thought we had died and gone to our eternal home. To make things even better, it was vacant and available for immediate occupancy. We could move in right away! The sale price of $67,000 was monumental compared to our former home of $7,500. Nevertheless, we decided to approach the owners and inquire as to the specifics.

At 3:00 p.m. on Christmas Eve, 1984, we met with the owners, Mr. and Mrs. O'Neal, a very sweet retired couple. They were hoping for a $14,000 down payment instead of our offer of $7,000, but, as I began to explain our ministry to them, they realized that we were a young couple with little means. They were so good to us, as the Lord touched their hearts, and they accepted our meager offer. They even agreed to carry the contract since the bank wouldn't "touch us with a ten-foot pole." We were so happy and elated knowing that the Lord had answered our prayers!

Mr. O'Neal told our real estate agent in passing, "If the Wheelers back out for some reason, don't you ever again bring us anyone who doesn't have a $14,000 down payment." After signing the contract, I was a nervous wreck. Our monthly house payment was going to be $639. Even to an evangelist living by faith, it seemed impossible! However, the Lord kept reassuring my heart that He would provide. Just before we were about to leave the negotiating table, my agent said, "Now, Richard and Marilyn, since tomorrow is Christmas, you will not have to come into the office because we will, obviously, be closed. But you will have to come in first thing the day after Christmas to give us an additional $800."

I was shocked and replied, "Why do we have to pay you $800?"

He told me, "You owe Mr. O'Neal for the remaining property taxes he prepaid since he assumed that he wasn't going to sell the house within the property tax year."

The whole thing sounded Greek to me. Marilyn noticed how pale my face began to turn. I was about ready to back out of the agreement when, once again, I heard the unmistakable voice of the Lord reassure me as He said, "I will provide."

We walked out to the car and, try as we might, we couldn't figure out where we were going to secure the additional money. We were stone-broke. "Oh well," we said, "the worst thing that can happen is that we will have to return to the office and tear up the contract and then continue looking for another home." From all outward appearances, it seemed that our dream home was a sand castle about to face an incoming high tide.

At 5:00 a.m. on Christmas day, the Lord stirred my spirit to seek Him in prayer, so I crawled out of our sleeping berth, which was above the cab of our motor home. Our girls were sleeping inside the Mendenhalls' home. I sat on the floor and just thanked the Lord for the celebration of Christmas even though I was a bit sorrowful that we didn't have money to purchase the gifts that we would have liked to give to our children.

As I continued to pray, I asked, "Lord, where are we going to find the money needed for the property tax that is due tomorrow morning?"

The Lord impressed upon me to remember my life verse, which is *"Trust in the LORD with all thine heart; and lean not unto thine own understanding. . . "* (Proverbs 3:5-6). He then told me to rent out the new home we were attempting to buy. I immediately latched onto this as being an excellent idea. Renting! I had never thought of it, and, since we were going to be heading out of Portland on the first of January for a three-month Southern California speaking tour, it seemed perfect! If we could just find someone who needed temporary housing, we could save up enough money to regain everything we had spent on our down payment to purchase the home. But I pondered, "Who?"

Quick as a wink, the Lord gave me the name of

Pastor Dwayne Driver. Pastor Dwayne was an old acquaintance whom I had met and come to know over the years from my youth pastor days in Port Orford. I had just spoken with him the week before at the Portland Foursquare Church during their Christmas program. He told me that he was doing a pioneer work in the inner city of Portland. In fact, his ministry was doing so well that he was moving a family in from Sisters, Oregon, to become associates alongside him and his wife. Pastor Dwayne had recounted to me how difficult it was to find a rental home for his future associates, Jim and Lucy. They had been looking for two months to no avail. I expressed my sorrow over the situation, and we parted that night from the church, never imagining that we would be playing a part in a drama in which God was planning to manifest and perform His mighty works.

I became very excited with the possibility that the Lord was presenting to me. However, I had one reservation. How was I going to share with Marilyn that I thought the Lord was leading me to rent out our new home to Jim and Lucy and that we would not move into it for at least three months, during which time, we would be traveling to minister? Now, keep in mind that this was my wife's dream home and I certainly didn't want to be a bearer of bad tidings on the joyous day of Christmas. I committed my dilemma to the Lord and got up from the floor to seek out Al Mendenhall so he could pray with me about it.

After Al and I prayed together, I was strengthened and at peace to go and face my wife. I needed to know how she would react to the idea of renting out her dream home. I opened the RV door and found that Marilyn was awake and that she had been in prayer. I carefully laid the entire scenario before her and then awaited her reaction. She proceeded to tell me her side of the story.

She told me, "Around 3:00 this morning, I woke up and slipped out of bed to seek the Lord in prayer."

I remembered hearing Marilyn stir, but, it being that time of the morning, I had remained anchored to the bed oblivious to what the Lord was doing with her.

She continued to explain, "During my prayer time, the Lord led me to Psalm 118:5-8, *'I called upon the Lord in distress: the LORD answered me, and set me in a large place. . . . It is better to trust in the LORD than to put confidence in man.'* To me, the *large* place is the home we are about to purchase and we need to depend on the Lord to provide for us."

It was obvious to us that we had nowhere to turn but to the Lord since we didn't know anyone who had the $800 we needed. I was astonished that the Lord had been speaking to her heart previously during the early morning hours about the matter. After reading the Scripture verse, we were blessed and assured that it was the Lord's leading to rent out our new home.

I waited until 9:00 that morning to call pastor Dwayne. Actually, it was amazing that I had even kept his phone number in my wallet for three whole days since the night we had spoken! I never keep papers or things that I can't imagine I'll ever need in the future. I happen to be one of those "neat freaks" who drive the people crazy who live with me. I am forever throwing things away in order to be rid of clutter. Whenever something is missing from around our home, I can hear the haunting words, "Dad," or "Richard, did you throw away such and such?" Unfortunately, about 95 percent of the time I have to confess, "Yes, I did." But there is always that 5 percent in which I can say, "No way—I wouldn't do that."

Pastor Dwayne was elated to hear the news and told me that he would send Jim right over from the motel where he and Lucy were staying to check out our new home. Within thirty minutes, Jim came over and introduced himself. After we exchanged greetings, Jim said, "This house will do just fine."

We laughed and told him that we weren't at the house that was for rent, but that we were just guests of the Mendenhalls. We explained that our new home was about two miles away from where we were and that we would drive him over to see the place. The Mendenhall and Wheeler children weren't too excited about the prospect, since they had to be patient and wait for us to return before they could exchange and open their Christmas gifts. Nevertheless, Al and I gave Jim the grand tour of the empty house, Marilyn and Sherie stayed with the children. When we were finished, we ended up in the basement where he said, "I would be delighted to rent your home on a temporary basis so that my wife and I could have time to look for a home to purchase within this same area."

He then began to recount the tale of what the Lord had been doing in his life during the move to Portland. Jim was an nurse anesthetist by profession and had been living and working in Sisters, Oregon. On one particular day, Pastor Dwayne had preached at Jim's church and shared about the ministry he was doing in the inner city of Portland. That night Jim and Lucy had felt mysteriously moved by the Lord to be a part of Pastor Dwayne's ministry. At the same time, Pastor Dwayne had been praying for an assistant associate pastor, so, they both began to earnestly seek the Lord for His guidance and approval. For Jim it was a major change. It meant leaving a secure job and the wilds of Central Oregon for the big city of Portland. In a nutshell, it meant selling out and moving by faith. Through prayer, he was able to hurdle most of the obstacles. However, all endeavors regarding the call to ministry seemed to bring insecurities of wondering whether or not it was *truly the will of God.*

While we were in the basement of our new home, Jim continued to share his testimony of how God, on their behalf, confirmed their decision to move to Portland and enter into ministry. Al and I were blessed to witness how the hand of the Lord had moved on behalf of Jim and Lucy. He told of the time when a total stranger came up to him and Lucy during a Sunday evening service and said, "I hope you don't think me to be forward as I am a stranger passing through town, but during the service I couldn't take my eyes off you. I felt that the Lord was prompting me to tell you that He realizes that you're feeling insecure about the changes in your life, but you need to move in the direction He is leading. This change you're involved in is ordered of the Lord for His will and His purpose."

Jim and Lucy were overwhelmed with awe that the Lord would encourage them with a messenger and a message to help establish them in their move to Portland. Thus, they began to spend their weekends looking for a house, which kept leading to a dead end. Weekend after weekend, nothing turned up, and, again, they became discouraged and doubted their calling. Again the Lord was faithful. About three weeks before Jim's job was to terminate in Sisters, Oregon, a Christian sister came up to them and told them, "The Lord has spoken to me in prayer and has revealed to me that you will not have to look for a house, because the Lord is going to have someone call you about a place to live."

Jim and Lucy thought that the word they had received was too great for their little faith because, as they explained to her, "We don't know a single person besides Pastor Dwayne and his wife who live in or near the city of Portland."

Both Pastor Dwayne and his wife were also perplexed as to the housing situation. They were of little use in helping Jim and Lucy to find a house. To add to the stakes, Jim and Lucy had housing requirements that made it much more difficult than usual to find a place. First, their home had to be in North Portland and within walking distance of Kaiser Hospital because they only had one car.

Secondly, their home had to have a fenced yard to allow their two German Short Hair Pointers. When we called Dwayne to tell Jim to come over and see the house we had for rent, you can imagine the hope and blessing Jim and Lucy received. What was incredible was that our home was within walking distance of the hospital *And* had a fenced yard *And*, since I have hunting blood in my veins, I loved pointers! God is so GOOD! By the time all three of us were through telling each other our stories, we were all wiping tears of joy. We all held hands that chilly Christmas morning and thanked God for His faithfulness in leading and providing for each of us.

Once we went outside, I gave Jim the key to our house and realized that, in our excitement, we had not discussed the rental amount. Upon the sale of our Port Orford home, we had received a down payment, and Gary was paying the balance owed to us via monthly payments. With this in mind, Marilyn and I had concluded that we needed at least $400 each month in order for us to make the monthly loan payment of $639 on our new home. So I told Jim that the rent would be $400 per month. Jim told me that $400 was *exactly* the amount that he and Lucy had agreed upon. He then, immediately whipped out his checkbook to write out the payment. I was so excited because I had half of the money we needed for the next morning and we only needed the Lord to provide $400 more.

As that glorious thought was running through my mind, Jim handed me the check and I glanced at it, expecting to see $400. However, to my surprise, I saw $800! In shock, I told Jim we had agreed upon $400, and he casually said, "I may as well throw in the last month's rental payment now."

With tears welling up in my eyes, I told Jim that we had needed to come up with $800 by 10:00 the next morning. We all stood there in awe of our merciful and loving God and how He had directed the events of that special and miraculous Christmas morning. Who would have ever imagined, that on a non-business day, the Lord would have conducted business with His people? God had confirmed the words that He had given Marilyn and me from the early morning hours of that day. What a delight it was for me to be able to walk up to my beloved wife, kiss her gently on the forehead, and, while presenting her with the $800 check, wish her a Merry Christmas and then tell her the Providential story of Jim and Lucy—our new tenants!

CHAPTER 30

There's No Place Like Home for the Holidays

A couple of days after that miraculous Christmas, we bid "adieu" to the Mendenhalls and headed out for Marilyn's parents' home which was in good old Santa Monica, California. There we spent the New Year's holiday and then began our ministry throughout Southern California. As we proceeded down the ramp onto Interstate 5 heading south in our RV, I distinctly recall hearing the Lord whisper to my inner man saying, "I will have the new home you have just purchased paid off within five years." It *was*, unmistakably, the voice of the Lord that I had grown to recognize.

Immediately, I shared with Marilyn what the Lord had told me and she gave me a look which said, "Sure—and fairy tales can come true, too."

We ministered throughout Southern California on our usual annual course. The expression "birds fly south for the winter" was our yearly moto. We figured it was only natural for us to head south to minister in a safe environment free of ice and snow which would make RV traveling less dangerous. We traveled and ministered until March, at which time we headed back north to our home in Portland, Oregon.

Both of Marilyn's parents were born in Scotland, and her dad was a typical frugal Scotsman to the "nth" degree. However, he was so happy when we came south for the winter that he let us make our base station at the apartment he owned. Upon our departure to Portland, he would often bless us with gas money for our return journey. This particular Christmas season continued to be more miraculous and overflowing with blessings from God. Marilyn's dad gave us an unexpected gift of $10,000 and told us we could put it toward the purchase of our new home! We were blessed to catch a glimpse of God's promise, *"....Eye hath not seen, nor ear heard, neither have entered into the heart of man, the things which God hath prepared for them that love him"* (I Corinthians 2:9). The gift was so far beyond our expectations that we could truly witness in our spirit Psalm 23:5-6, which says, *"....My cup runneth over. Surely goodness and mercy shall follow me all the days of my life. . . ."*

While we were traveling back home to Portland, the Lord revealed to me that He had caused Mr. Cobb's heart to bestow such a generous gift upon us so we could glorify Him. We were to deposit the money into the house account toward the down payment. It would be a testimony of God's goodness and, at the same time, be a blessing to the O'Neals, especially since they didn't expect it! The Lord wanted to bless the O'Neals because they had ministered to us by agreeing to forgo the down payment they had wanted. Our Heavenly Father is exceedingly good to those who are kind to His children. This is why the Scripture says, *"Inasmuch as ye have done it unto one of these the least of these my brethren, ye have done it unto me"* (Matthew 25:40).

For several years, our ministry took us throughout the Pacific Northwest and Southwest speaking at children's camps and crusades, school assemblies (both, public and private), and churches of all denominations.

Seminary could have never taught me the many lessons I learned while ministering to children. The Lord gave me discernment and an insight to youth, their homes, and, more importantly, their parents. The early years of ministry enabled me to develop Mantle Ministries into what it is today.

Speaking of Mantle Ministries, that wasn't the name with which we began. In the early days, we were named Little Bear, Mountain Man, Pilgrim Productions. As we expanded our messages and costumes to include a deeper understanding of our American heritage, we began to use American Heritage Ministries. However, sometime later, we discovered that American Heritage was already a legal registered name owned by another corporation. After much prayer, we felt led to name our ministry Mantle Ministries. Our hope is to share the vision of God's blessing and anointing on this once great nation and our responsibility to carry the mantle forward so that we may pass it on to the next generation. This mantle will be the task of preserving our God-given Christian heritage, which was established through faith in Jesus Christ by our Founding Fathers.

"And it came to pass, as they still went on, and talked, that, behold, there appeared a chariot of fire, and horses of fire, and parted them both asunder; and Elijah went up by a whirlwind into heaven. And Elisha saw it, and he cried, My father, my father, the chariot of Israel, and the horsemen thereof. And he saw him no more: and he took hold of his own clothes, and rent them in two pieces.

He took up also the mantle of Elijah that fell from him, and went back, and stood by the bank of Jordan; And he took the mantle of Elijah that fell from him, and smote the

waters, and said, Where is the LORD God of Elijah?...."
(1 Kings 2:11-14).

CHAPTER 31

How to Establish a Fruitful Ministry

Before leaving Port Orford, and while on a prayer walk in 1979, I distinctly recall how shocked I was when I received the news regarding one of my former Bible instructors. I had grown to love and admire the man immensely. However, he committed adultery, divorced his wife, and ran off with one of his former Bible seminary students. I couldn't believe it! The instructor had been well-grounded in the Word of God, so I was totally dismayed. I asked the Lord in prayer how this came to be. The Lord quickly responded by His Spirit to my spirit saying, "This, too, could happen to you."

My response was not, "Oh, not me, Lord; I would *never* do such a stupid thing." Instead, I answered, "Yes, Lord; if this can happen to one of the most accomplished, well-studied and best Bible communicators in the world that I have ever had the privilege of sitting under, then it *could* certainly happen to me!" I recalled what II Peter 3:17 said, *"Ye, therefore, beloved, seeing that ye know these things before, beware lest ye also, being led away with the error of the wicked, fall from your own stedfastness."*

I pleaded, "But, Lord: I don't want this to happen to me!" In further despair, I cried out to the Lord asking Him, "What can I do to keep myself from falling into gross sin?"

The Lord spoke to my heart and said, "You must keep in prayer and in My Word, seek Me daily, and continually stay close to Me."

The answer seemed so simple to me. Yet, as I began to practice rising each morning at 4:00 so that I could pray, study His Word, and fast on a weekly basis, I soon discovered the difficulties of the Christian life.

Jesus Christ, Himself, warned us, *"Watch and pray, that ye enter not into temptation: the spirit indeed is willing, but the flesh is weak"* (Matthew 26:41).

After several years of such a rigorous schedule and austere discipline in Bible reading and fasting, I began to experience signs of stress. My body was so hyped up that a heart attack or even death could have resulted, so I asked the Lord if He would release me of my rigorous schedule. Especially, I wanted to be released amidst touring. Instead, I asked Him if He would allow me to rise up at 6:00 a.m. to study and pray until 7:30 a.m. for five days a week. I sensed that He nodded with approval and, by God's grace, I have been able to keep this new pace for the past fifteen years. It has kept me, just as God had promised.

The Lord seized me with this Bible text that has remained constantly in my mind throughout my Christian walk:

"And take heed to yourselves, lest at any time your hearts be overcharged with surfeiting, and drunkenness, and cares of this life, and so that day come upon you unawares. For as a snare shall it come on all them that dwell on the face of the whole earth. Watch ye therefore, and pray always that ye may be accounted worthy to escape all these things that shall come to pass, and to stand before the Son of man" (Luke 21:34-36).

I thought being a Christian was a piece of cake during the early years of my Christian walk. I felt so free! I loved grace, especially since I had gone through practicing seven different religions which only left me depressed as a result of their inability to deliver me from my sins and bring me into the love of Almighty God. It felt so good to know that I didn't have a Heavenly Father who was going to beat me over the head with a big stick every time I did something wrong. However, God was training me to seek His will for my life as Paul so aptly wrote in Philippians,

"Wherefore, my beloved, as ye have always obeyed, not as in my presence only, but now much more in my absence, work out your own salvation with fear and trembling. For it is God, which worketh in you both to will and to do of His good pleasure" (Philippians 2:12-13).

As I grew and matured over the years, I came to realize that the Christian life is a life of sacrifice and self-denial—the Cross. Constantly, I must die to myself so I can live to love, serve, and please Christ Jesus. However, I do realize that I cannot earn my salvation by doing works, because as my salvation was paid by the atoning blood of the Lamb, Jesus Christ. *"For by grace are ye saved through faith; and not of yourselves: it is the gift of God: Not of works, lest any man should boast"* (Ephesians 2:8-9).

I was consistently striving to love my Lord and Savior more each day and, because of that, I began to change with respect to many little things that I had done in the past which were not expedient in making me fit for my

Master's use. I find that Psalm 19 is a wonderful chapter on which to meditate regarding the balance of works versus grace. The following verse serves as a keystone for my life and my desire to serve Christ: *"Keep back thy servant also from presumptuous sins; let them not have dominion over me: then shall I be upright, and I shall be innocent from the great transgression"* (Psalm 19:13). An example that serves well to explain how the Lord led me to a higher walk and taught me to discern between His grace and my responsibility follows.

One evening, I decided to take Marilyn on a date to a movie theater. It had been over three years since we had been to a movie. The last movie that we had seen was *The American Tale.* Generally, we were too busy to frequent movie theaters, so we decided to see a movie that was highly recommended by Christians. By that experience, I learned *not* to trust the judgment of others. Rather, I need to seek the Lord and His judgment. We arrived in plenty of time to have a walk around the lobby. We were amazed at how many people were in the multi-theater. I surveyed the billboards for the featured movies, and I was appalled. I began to realize the depths to which this nation had plunged into wickedness and ungodliness. Have you ever been in a place where you felt as if you didn't fit in or got the "creeps"? That was exactly how I was feeling when I walked into that lobby. We quickly headed to our scheduled show, *The Last of the Mohicans.*

As we sat waiting for the movie to start, previews of coming attractions were being shown. The previews started with huge white letters that read, "The following previews have been edited for general audiences." We soon found that we must not be very "general" since we found the previews to be sensual, graphic, and too violent.

Thus, we decided to wait outside the door until the previews were completed. While waiting outside, several local youth from our home school community came by and noticed us standing by the door. I was a bit embarrassed to be seen in a movie theater. I was really uncomfortable being in a place where I felt the habitation of demons. I was also wondering, "What movie could those young teens be going to view?" My suspicion was great since most of the movies in the theater were not suitable for human viewing.

Early the next morning while in devotion, I had a chance to spend some time in prayer. I felt an immense sorrow for having gone to the theater. I had never felt that way before. I felt defiled. I began to confess my feelings and apologized to the Lord for having gone to the theater. The Lord revealed to me why I felt the way I did. He led me to several verses such as *"And grieve not the Holy Spirit of God, whereby ye are sealed unto the day of redemption"* (Ephesians 4:30) and *"...I will behave myself wisely in a perfect way. O when wilt thou come unto me? I will walk within my house with a perfect heart. I will set no wicked thing before mine eyes: I hate the work of them that turn aside; it shall not cleave to me. . . ." (Psalm 101:3).*

I was in mourning because I had grieved the Holy Spirit of the living God that dwelt within me. Needless to say, after confessing and repenting, I made a vow to never, again, set foot into a theater. *"If we confess our sins, He is faithful and just to forgive us our sins, and to cleanse us from all unrighteousness"* (I John 1:9).

My decision was not based on compulsion, rather, it was because of my love for Christ and my desire to live holy before Him. Obviously, I am not yet completely holy, nor do I ever expect to be on this side of Glory. However, like Paul and as long as there is breath in my body, I will *"...press toward the mark for the prize of the high calling of God in Christ Jesus"* (Philippians 3:14).

CHAPTER 32

My Eyes Have Seen the Light and the Glory

Immediately upon being born-again, I was so hungry for the Word of God that I literally spent hours each day reading, studying, and memorizing God's Word. As a result, God's Word penetrated my soul and I began to feel a burden for America and the direction it was heading. I was drawn to the hearts of the Old Testament prophets and their writings. My love for these prophets inflamed my fervor for proclaiming warnings of judgment on our nation. *The Late Great Planet Earth* greatly influenced my thinking and fueled my fervor even more. I was fanatical with such an urgency to preach the Second Coming of Jesus Christ. "Rapture fever" was my plight, and I was overbearing in my efforts of persuasion when sharing my faith. With vehemence, I expounded upon the Second Coming of Christ and the coming judgment upon this nation and the world. However, as I continued to mature and grow in the knowledge and grace of Jesus Christ, I began to become more balanced in regard to the Word of God.

Our move to Port Orford was used by the Lord to thrust me into another phase of ministry. Because of the Royal Rangers' camping program, I began to plan Bible messages for the boys at our outpost meetings. My previous twenty-three years of studying and knowledge of the Old West, cowboys, Indians, gunfighters, soldiers, and gold diggers had given me plenty of material to teach in a unique way while blending in Biblical and historical examples. In the beginning of this phase of our ministry, I had created three outfits to wear—my hand stitched-buckskin outfit with the bead work, and a Reformation monk robe and a Puritan outfit, which Marilyn helped me sew. Before long, I felt led of the Lord to create costumes for each period of history that I covered in my messages. It didn't take long before six authentic outfits were created.

Providentially, in 1979, I read *The Light and the Glory,* co-authored by Reverend Peter Marshall and David Manuel. God used this book to lead me into even another phase of our ministry. Up until that time, my messages did not include God's providence in the forming and shaping of America. You may ask, "Why?" The answer is simple. I hadn't received any teaching or understanding of the historical and providential hand of God upon this nation. After all, I had attended the typical godless government schools of our land that have stripped the providence of God from our textbooks and classroom teachings for the past one hundred years. Reading *The Light and the Glory* and the insights of the authors elated me. The idea that God had a direct hand in the founding of America caused me to become so excited that I soon began to incorporate the providence message into our ministry and add more period costumes.

Another major providential occurrence took place during this time. I had been ministering in Albany, Oregon, when I happened to notice a circular ad on the church bulletin board inviting people to attend a "Founding of America" seminar to be held by a minister named Marshall Foster, founder of the Mayflower Institute. The meeting was to held at the Portland Foursquare Church which was about a two-hour drive from Albany. Surprised, I immediately recognized the name of Marshall Foster. Marshall Foster had been a former instructor of mine, back in 1974, when I had attended *The Light and Power House* Bible Seminary in Westwood Village, California. I was interested in the seminar because it was designed to teach the principles of our nation's Christian roots. The opportunity to see and visit with Marshall made the trip even more attractive.

We arrived too late to catch the actual seminar since we had to finish ministering in Albany and then drive to Portland. However, I did get to speak with Marshall, and we rejoiced at the renewal of our friendship. To this day, our relationship thrives. I reintroduced Marshall to Marilyn introduced and my two girls, to him whom he had never met. Marshall shared with me that, after he left his teaching position in Westwood Village, he had moved to San Francisco to study under two Godly, elderly ladies, Miss Verna Hall and Miss Rosalie Slater. Under their instruction, Marshall Foster learned to research the documents of our Founding Fathers, and he became a master teacher in the understanding and origins of our nation's Christian heritage.

Marshall and Mary Elaine Swanson wrote a book called *The American Covenant (The Untold Story).* The Lord used the book as a tool to further enhance the call upon my life. You may wonder why I have bothered to spend so much time on this subject of who's who and all the seemingly superfluous details. It is because these are the major events that the Lord used to direct my steps for His glory and to make Mantle Ministries what He intended it to be. Under the influence of Peter Marshall and Marshall Foster, I began to delve into a massive study of the lost and forgotten covenant that the Lord made with the Pilgrim Fathers who established a beachhead in America for the Kingdom of God in 1620. Governor William Bradford so aptly put it in his writings of the period:

> *Last and not least, they cherished a great hope and inward zeal of laying good foundations, or at least of making some way towards it, for the propagation and advancement of the gospel of the kingdom of Christ in the remote parts of the world, even though they should be but stepping stones to others in the performance of so great a work.*

I couldn't find enough to read on this lost and forgotten covenant, so, as we traveled throughout the Unites States, I began to search for out-of-print books that had been printed in the 1800s. Within a few years, I had purchased hundreds of books: biographies, history, moral character builders, and Godly fiction. I acquired documentation of the faith of our Founding Fathers, and I began to see the need to republish and share these one-of-a-kind books. I began to look into the possibility of republishing books and found that such a project was much too costly for our faith ministry. Since I had covenanted with God not to solicit funds, we were not supported on a monthly basis by anyone. Thus, I had a dilemma: How could I republish these books without asking for money from those on our growing mailing list? I was left with only one choice, and that was to pray, pray, and pray again until the Lord gave me direction. Those years of prayer were a time of God's unique and unfolding plan for Mantle Ministries.

CHAPTER 33

A Legacy to Our Children

Through those years of prayer, God allowed two significant events to occur in our lives that began to motivate me to establish a foundation. The foundation was to support the preservation of my nation for my children's sake, to raise a Godly heritage, and to expand the message of our ministry.

The first event took place during the time of Christian singer and songwriter Keith Green's death in July of 1982. At the time, I was an associate pastor in Port Orford working with the youth. On a fair and sunny day, I decided to do some minor roof repair. While working on the roof, a youth I had been discipling, Troy Anderson, came running up excitedly and looked up to tell me he had just heard that Keith Green had died in a private plane crash at his ministry headquarters in Lindvale, Texas. Keith Green was a young talented musician who had profoundly influenced my life.

The first time I remember him ministering was in 1979 at a large outdoor Christian conference in Salem, Oregon. Our church had gone to the week-long event for a time of enrichment and fellowship. On Wednesday of that week, Marilyn, little Noelle, baby Aimee, and I showed up to hear the keynote speaker who was to be followed by Keith Green. After the speaker finished delivering his message, Keith stepped out onto the stage, smiled, waved, and proceeded to sit at the piano amidst the frantic cheers of his fans. As he began to sing his first song, several people in the crowd stood up from sitting on their blankets that were scattered on the grass throughout the outdoor amphitheater. They worked their way up toward the stage, stepping over fellow Christians who were still sitting, just to get a close-up picture of Keith at the piano. Dusk was approaching, and the camera flashes were popping one after the other. Right in the middle of his song, Keith stopped. He stood to his feet and approached the apron of the stage and said, "Put your idol boxes away. I am here to worship Jesus in music, and your cameras are distracting! Why do Christians get saved and delivered from sin and idolatry only to make idols of your favorite musicians? This is wrong! Let's get back to worship!"

As you can well imagine, you could have heard a pin drop in that crowd of several thousand people. I felt embarrassed for those standing with their cameras. Keith was a very non-compromising Christian, both, in his Bible teaching and in the words of his music. He definitely had a prophetic nature about his spirit and, although at first it caused me to stumble, I could well identify with his type of ministry since I, too, felt I possessed the same nature. It is a "turn or burn" kind of personality. I followed Keith's ministry for several years, bought his music, and kept abreast of what he and his wife, Melody, were doing by way of ministry. Needless to say, when Keith was killed suddenly, while in the middle of a sound and thriving ministry, I was shocked. I spent several days grieving over the sorrowful event.

One day as I was in prayer, I began to question the Lord about His way of doing things, especially when they didn't seem to make any sense. I asked the Lord, "Why would You take Keith Green so suddenly when his ministry was having such a great effect on people?"

The Lord answered me in a most unusual way by saying, "You, too, could die just as suddenly!"

I responded, "Not *I* Lord! I am too young to die, and my house is not in order. I don't want to die yet. Please give me some more time to establish my children before You call me home through death."

My thoughts were not that I was afraid to die. Rather, my thoughts were that I needed more time to teach my children God's commandments, statutes, and judgments. I wanted to make sure that my children were prepared to possess the land that God promised when He commanded us as parents to teach these things in Deuteronomy 6:1. I wanted my children to have HIS BLESSINGS and PROMISES!

As I began to meditate upon the possibility of an untimely death, it occurred to me that, if I did die suddenly, Marilyn would most likely remarry. My feelings in regard to the possibility of her remarrying were not those of jealousy but of remorse. I knew deep down in my heart that, even if she married a mature believer, he most likely would not possess the precious knowledge of our American Christian history or that of our Founding Fathers, especially from a Christian perspective. I had found various passages in the Bible that commanded fathers to instruct their children in the knowledge of their heritage. I also read what God had done to establish their nation.

*"Give ear, O my people, to my law:
incline your ears to the words of my mouth.
I will open my mouth in a parable: I will
utter dark sayings of old: Which we have
heard and known, and our fathers have told
us. We will not hide them from their
children, shewing to the generation to come
the praises of the LORD, and His strength,
and His wonderful works that He hath done.
For He established a testimony in Jacob,
and appointed a law in Israel, which He
commanded our fathers, that they should
make them known to their children: That the
generation to come might know them, even
the children which should be born; who
should arise and declare them to their
children: That they might set their hope in
God, and not forget the works of God, but
keep his commandments: And might not be
as their fathers, a stubborn and rebellious
generation; a generation that set not their
heart aright, and whose spirit was not
stedfast with God"* (Psalm 78:1-8).

Besides not having fully taught my children their
heritage, I realized that I had not drawn up a will. I just
figured there was no purpose in having a will since I had
nothing to will to my family. I was, at the time and
momentarily speaking, stone-broke. Yet the Lord made me
see that *"a little that a righteous man hath is better than
the riches of many wicked"* (Psalm 37:16). It was at this
point, the Lord instructed me to realize that a will involved
much more than having money or property to leave to my

wife and children. God inspired me to pass a heritage onto my family in, primarily, two ways.

First, I could leave my family a testimony of my life and the mighty deeds that the Lord had done to bring me to the point of salvation. I recognized that I was a poor excuse for a writer, so what could I do? *"....[His] grace is sufficient for [me]; for [His] strength is made perfect in weakness. Most gladly therefore will I rather glory in my infirmities, that the power of Christ may rest upon me"* (II Corinthians 12:9). This led me to decide to record the "Little Bear Story" on audio cassette. I was so excited that I went out and purchased a micro-cassette recorder and, over a period of two weeks, I recorded everything that I felt was necessary for my children to know about their father in the event of an untimely death. After having accomplished that feat and finding that I was still alive, I began the second phase of leaving my will.

The second way for me to leave my heritage was made possible when the Lord provided for me to buy a mini-recording studio. I was able to set up a studio in which I could make recordings while traveling and ministering on the road–even when we stayed at a hosting family's house or in a church room. I began recording the Christian heritage of the founding of America from the time period of the Reformation up to the late 1800s. The project took about two years. As a result, my "Historical Devotional" cassette series was birthed. I never dreamed that those cassette stories would, someday, be sold throughout the U.S.A. to families for their children to listen to me retell what God did to establish this nation! At the time, I had a very limited evangelistic ministry. *"For who hath despised the day of small things? for they shall rejoice . . ."* (Zechariah 4:10).

After the recording project was completed, I thanked the Lord for keeping me alive long enough to have completed the task. The fact was that, since I had worked so hard to achieve my goal of recording my testimony and the twelve volumes of "Historical Devotionals," I could hardly wait to die! I knew if I died, I could rest assured that, if Marilyn did remarry, my children wouldn't have to depend on a step-father to instruct them in the founding of America since they would have the "Historical Devotional" cassettes narrated by their very own father! I pray that, Lord willing, my children will share them with their own children–my grandchildren! Knowing that I had fulfilled the admonishments of Psalms 44, 78, and 107, I *"delighted in the law of the Lord"* (Psalm 1:2).

I took delight in the fact that my children could literally say unto the Lord, *"We have heard with our ears, O God, our fathers have told us, what work thou didst in their days, in the times of old"* (Psalm 44:1).

"We have heard and known, and our fathers have told us. We will not hide them from their children, shewing to the generation to come the praises of the LORD, and His strength, and His wonderful works that He hath done . . . That the generation to come might know them, even the children which should be born; who should arise and declare them to their children: That they might set their hope in God, and not forget the works of God, but keep His commandments" (Psalm 78:3-4, 6-7).

"Oh that men would praise the LORD for His goodness, and for His wonderful works to the children of men!" (Psalm 107:8).

162

Even though my project appeared to be completed, I began to entertain the idea of video-taping as many of my messages as possible for my family before I died. After all, idleness is the "workshop of the devil." I prayed about the video project and asked the Lord to direct me in my new vision. I felt the need to begin the project, but I ran into one difficulty after another. I wasn't sure if the opposition was coming from God or from the enemy, who was trying to hinder me. I recall that, one time while speaking in Washington, I had hired a professional camera crew to come out to videotape one of my presentations. The event was so unsuccessful that after the meeting the crew refused to take any money from me. In fact, they apologized to me and told me they had never, in all their years of business, encountered so much trouble as they did with my taping. Furthermore, not one single word of what I had said turned out on their video master! I just smiled as though I had expected the news. I ran into so much trouble that I let the video vision die for a season. God later resurrected it in His timing, as you will see during the course of His unfolding drama in my life story.

CHAPTER 34

God Answers Prayer

Do you ever think about a dear old friend from your past whom you've lost track of? Do you often wonder whatever became of him or her? I can imagine that most everyone has had this experience at some point in his or her life. If you recall my account of my Santa Monica Beach days, during my junior and senior high school years, I had a few close buddies named Randy Como, Mark Pellet, and Billy Davis. I also hung out with Andrew Meyers, Dennis Thompson, and a guy named Bart. Since I had a hard time fitting in with the wild and crazy bunch of the 1960s, I had few friends. My somewhat quiet and reserved nature was very cautious of bad company, so I was thankful that the Lord allowed me a few close friends while growing up. We were fortunate that we all lived within three blocks of each other and got to chum around together all year long.

Naturally, when I grew up and married and then moved away, I always wondered what had become of my close friends. So I decided to look them up while I was ministering in Southern California–my old stomping grounds. After some research, I found Mark Pellet, who led me to finding Dennis Thompson since he had married Mark's sister. It was a great reunion, and we had the wonderful opportunity to reminisce over old times. It's amazing to see what time does to the face and stature of our youth. Mark introduced me to his children who were almost the age we were when we had hung out together as friends on the beach. Oh, how time had flown!

We pondered on the whereabouts of Billy Davis, but none of us could find a trace of him. To me, this was disconcerting. I could not be content to let his situation remain unknown, so I earnestly began to find him. In fact, I searched so earnestly that I believe British explorer Sir Henry Morton Stanley, who found Dr. David Livingstone, the missionary explorer in Africa, would be very proud of my efforts!

My last contact with Billy had been after he had returned from Vietnam in 1970. We were grateful to be able to get reacquainted, but it was obvious that Vietnam had left some serious and negative effects on Billy. Thus, continuing a close friendship with him seemed very unlikely at the time. Our paths, once again parted with each of us going in separate directions. I married and moved to Oregon.

Twenty years later in 1990, I became so curious and burdened to find Billy that I began to have dreams that I found him and would then wake up only to find I had not. I just couldn't shake him off my mind, so I began praying that the Lord would give me wisdom to find him. After praying month after month to seemingly no avail, I suddenly felt the Lord inspire me to call the California State Motor Vehicles Department in Sacramento. It was astounding that I could remember Billy's middle name and date of birth, especially since twenty years had transpired since our last encounter. I think that it was even more remarkable since many men can scarcely remember their own wedding anniversary or their children's birthdays! Remembering that valuable information enabled me to have the Motor Vehicles Department do a trace for me. They were able to tell me that Billy had turned in his California driver's license many years prior, but they couldn't help me with any further information. It dawned on me that if *they* could give me that kind of information, I could contact other states and make inquiries. So I contacted South Carolina since it was the state of his birth, but that led to a dead end. I then proceeded to contact several other southern states by phone, which also ended in disappointment. Since Billy had been in the armed services, I decided to contact the Veteran's Administration Hospital in California to see if they had any record of him needing medical services. That was another dead end, but I knew Billy had to be somewhere! Even the hit song, "Somewhere Out There" from the movie *The American Tale* urged my heart on. The song was playing everywhere on the radio, in the malls, and at many other places. Every time I heard that song, I would get all choked up and pray that the Lord would continue to help me find Billy.

Scarcely a month would go by that I didn't petition the Lord to help me find Billy. I felt like the widow who earnestly and persistently went to the unjust judge for action to be taken on her behalf. Jesus had used the parable to demonstrate the need for men to continue praying and not faint (Luke 18:1-8).

Finally, my determined prayer began to pay off! By Providence, we purchased a house for my mother from a man who just so happened to work for the Portland police department. I asked him how police officers traced people, and he told me that they used a computer. He further explained that the computer searched for data that linked the name of an individual with the date of his or her birth. I asked him to please help me find Billy using the computer, and he consented. After several days, I called him, and he told me that, although he had searched several states throughout America, he hadn't found anything. To say the least, I was sorely disappointed, and again I continued to pray.

Two months passed by when I decided to call him back again and ask him to *please* try searching more states. He told me that my timing couldn't have been any better since the computer technology had just been improved and their computer system could now search entire sections of the country—all at one time.

About three days later, he called to tell me that he had located a man named Billy Lee Davis who was six feet tall, 190 pounds with light hair, and blues eyes with a birth date of February 28, 1947. As he spoke, my heart was racing with excitement, and I responded with, "Yes! That's him!"

Five years of earnest prayer was finally paying off. *"The effectual fervent prayer of a righteous man availeth much"* (James 5:16b). The police officer proceeded to tell me that Billy lived in Denver, Colorado, and gave me his address. You can only imagine how much I thanked him!

I called a Denver information operator and asked if they could give me Billy's phone number. Sadly, the only answer I received was the unwelcome news, "I'm sorry, but that phone number is unlisted."

"Can you make a special exception?" I asked. She only gave me another negative response. I hung up the phone and dialed again hoping to get a different operator whom I could persuade. The second operator responded exactly as the first, so I asked if she would verify the address I had so I could write a letter. Once again, I was given no information. Seeming to be so close and yet so far, again I went to the Lord in prayer for several days wondering what to do.

After about a week, I felt led, once again, to call another information operator. The operator wouldn't give me the number even though I tried to convince him that Billy was like a long-lost brother. I pleaded. The operator told me that he could lose his job if he gave me the phone number, so I asked him if he would verify the address I had, and he still answered, "No." Silently, I prayed and asked God to change the operator's heart, and to my pleasant surprise, the operator asked me, "What address do you have for Mr. Billy Davis?"

This was the first operator who had shown even an inkling of concern for my plight! Of course, I gave the operator the address I had received from the police officer. The operator responded by telling me, "You're close, but you are one number off."

Eagerly, I asked, "Could you tell me what the missing number is?"

He answered, "Not exactly, but you are off a number between one and ten."

I then said, "If I begin to count one through ten, will you affirm the number when I say it?" He agreed. I slowly began to count, "One, two, three, four, five, six, seven . . . "

"That's it," he said.

Ecstatic and with pure joy, I profusely thanked the operator and blessed him in the name of Jesus. Finally, I had the address I needed for the following letter:

October 14, 1990

Dear Billy,

For some time I have tried to contact you and see how you're doing. I hope that you remember me, your old neighborhood pal and school buddy from when you lived in Santa Monica, California, back in the 1960s. I trust that you are well. I have been thinking of you for many months, and I have been praying for the Lord to lead me to find you. Please write me and let me know if you have received this letter.

Your friend,

Richard Wheeler

I sent the letter, and with bated breath, I waited to see if Billy would write back. With eager anticipation, day after day, I checked the mail and found not a single word from Billy. Days turned into weeks, and, when the weeks turned into months, I became perplexed as to why Billy hadn't replied to my letter. I concluded that Billy may have not responded for several reasons. Perhaps he had moved and left no forwarding address, or maybe he had forgotten who I was (after all, it had been twenty years since we had last seen each other). Another reason may be that he did remember me but had no interest in seeing me. What could I do? I had come so close, but I was so far from seeing him.

God is so faithful. Again, Providence came to my rescue. It just so happened that I was scheduled to fly to New York to be the keynote speaker at the state homeschool convention. So I figured that since my connecting flight would be in Denver anyway that I ought to leave a day early, rent a car, check into a motel, and then try to find the street on which Billy lived. I could just casually stop by and say, "I happened to be in the neighborhood."

I executed my idea just as I had planned. I found myself in Denver with a city street map plotting my course to Billy's house, which was in Arvada, a suburb of Denver. I drove up to his house in my rental car and noticed that the lights were on, so I took that as an indication that he was home. I walked up to the door and knocked. A lady answered the door, and I said, "Is this the home of Billy Lee Davis, born in Greenville, South Carolina, February 28, 1947, and whose mother is Pinky Davis?" With a name like Pinky, I knew there could be only one Billy Davis who would fit the description.

With some hesitation, the lady said, "Yes."

I'm sure she must have thought that I was some kind of undercover detective, so I told her that I was Richard Wheeler and that Billy and I had been friends back in our good old school days. Seemingly somewhat relieved, she invited me inside.

"Hi, my name is Jennifer, and I am Billy's wife," she said. "I'll check to see if Billy is awake. It's about time for him to be getting up, as he has to get ready to go to work. He works the night-shift at a local plant."

I was a bit nervous since I didn't know whether or not Billy would view me as an unwelcome intruder to his life. It seemed as if I waited for an eternity before Billy came out of the bedroom where he was getting ready for work. When he finally did come out, he had a big winsome smile that confirmed to his wife and to me that he found joy in seeing me. He looked at me and said, "Richard Wheeler! My goodness gracious, how in the world did you find me and show up here at my door?"

With tears in my eyes, I stood up and hugged him and then briefly told him of the tale and trail that I had followed and how the Lord led me to his house. Billy was overwhelmed and amazed with wonder at God's providence in directing my steps to him. He told me that, when he had received my letter several months earlier, he was at one of the lowest points of his life. He was receiving medical treatment and was so emotionally down that he didn't have the strength even to acknowledge my letter. He was touched to think that I had remembered him after all those years had passed. Then he said, "Richard, your letter gave me hope to think that someone cared enough and loved me enough to remember me. I realized that the good Lord sent me your letter as a lifeline in my time of depression to help lift me up out of my despair."

Wow! Our God is awesome! At that moment, I understood why the Lord had placed such a burden on my heart to pray for Billy all those months before finding him.

"We can do all things through Christ who strengthens us" and "our God shall supply all our needs according to His riches and glory by Christ Jesus"(see Philippians 4:13, 19). God answers prayer!

Another significant event occurred during this time of my life. My wife Marilyn was expecting our third child!

CHAPTER 35

Children Are an Heritage of the Lord

Tragically, I have been raised in a generation that sells us a "bill of goods." One of the spoiled goods is that family planning is a decision to be made by a husband and wife without considering God's supreme desire. I was deceived into thinking that having "too many" children was a burden, an inconvenience in this day and age, and that an American family should be content with having only two children. At one time, I really believed that if a couple was set on having a large family then three children ought "to fill the bill of goods."

Consequently, I was happy and content with having just our two daughters, Noelle and Aimee. But Marilyn always longed for a third child. This left me with the responsibility of making sure that there were no "accidents" that would result in our having another child. Logically, I concluded that, since we were a traveling evangelistic family who toured in the small living quarters of a motor home, we were justified in restricting the size of our family to only two children.

There is an old Jewish proverb that says, "Man makes plans, and God laughs." God has a way of circumventing foolish people's best-laid plans. *"No purpose or plan of God can be thwarted"* (Job 42:2). I soon discovered this truth when I learned of the imminent birth of our third child whom, at the time, I did not want! I just couldn't imagine how I was going to emotionally handle a third child with my limited income and busy evangelist schedule. Since God had made other plans for me, He set into motion events that would prepare my spirit before my son, Joshua, was to be born. *"The preparations of the heart in man, and the answer of the tongue, is from the LORD"* (Proverbs 16:1). I didn't recognize it at the time, but God's hand was doing surgery on my obstinate heart which would cause me to repent of my "small family" mentality.

While we were ministering in Montana, during the summer of 1985, I began to see the hand of God prepare me for the conception of Joshua. In mid June, I was ministering at the Assembly of God church in Circle, Montana. In my usual manner, I knelt to pray prior to the service. The Spirit of the Lord poured out upon me and reached down into my spirit to such a depth that I became broken.

> *"A merry heart maketh a cheerful countenance: but by sorrow of the heart the spirit is broken. The heart of him that hath understanding seeketh knowledge: but the mouth of fools feedeth on foolishness"* (Proverbs 15:13-14).

I wept and groaned almost uncontrollably. I realized that the Lord was doing some major internal work, because my feelings and emotions were nearly beyond control.

After a period of time, I got up and, although I wasn't totally aware of what the Lord was doing, I committed myself to His sovereign care. After leaving Circle, we headed for White Sulfur Springs, Montana, to hold a Royal Rangers powwow where I was scheduled to be the camp speaker for a week. After the last night of ministering, I got up early and went on my prayer walk amongst the beautiful mountains of Central Montana. It was June 18, 1985.

I took my Bible with me on the walk, and I felt impressed to read Isaiah 44:1-4.

> *"Yet now hear, O Jacob my servant; and Israel, whom I have chosen: Thus saith the LORD that made thee, and formed thee from the womb, which will help thee; Fear not, O Jacob, my servant; and thou, Jesurun, whom I have chosen. For I will pour water upon him that is thirsty, and floods upon the dry ground: I will pour my spirit upon thy **seed**, and my blessing upon thine offspring: And they shall spring up as among the grass, as willows by the water courses."*

At the time, I thought the Lord was trying to tell me that He was going to increase the seed and fruit of my *ministry*. I was oblivious to what the Lord really had in mind when He showed me that passage in Isaiah.

After my prayer walk, we packed up our RV and headed out on our trip north towards Great Falls, Montana. I located the church where I was to minister the next morning for the Sunday service and parked the RV in its parking lot. That night, when our two daughters were tucked into bed and sound asleep, Marilyn and I found time to spend with each other.

One evening, about a month later, while we were in Hungry Horse, Marilyn informed me that she believed she was expecting our *third* child. I couldn't believe the words! They hit me like a ton of bricks. All I could say to her was, "How and when?" We calculated that our child must have been conceived, of all places, in the Great Falls church parking lot! Shocked and accusingly, I told Marilyn, "You deceived me!"

Holding her head high and with a big grin, she said, "Yes, I did, and I'm proud that we're going to have another baby."

I was sick, afraid, worried, and couldn't sleep. There I was, holding children's meetings for three weeks in a row throughout the state of Montana, under the supposition that I loved children. And I did. But having another child of my very own to care for and be responsible for was a *whole* other story! I had prayed every moment that I could that God would NOT allow this to happen to me! I was distraught and in anguish.

During that summer, while we were at Hungry Horse, our friends the Mendenhalls decided to come visit us for summer vacation. When they arrived, Marilyn and I told them of the news that we were expecting another child. Naturally, as I had expected them to be, they were elated. Anyone who was "touched" enough in the head to have four children *had* to be happy at such news, or so I thought. Everyone went into fits of joy and slapped each other on the back. Their four children plus our two girls danced with glee trying to decide what to name our child who was only one month old in the womb. I was fit to be tied. However, I did try with all my might to appear as happy as a lark.

Well, you can fool some people. But you can't fool friends. The following morning, Al and I went for a long walk to talk about ministry and the things of the Lord. Al said, "I suspect that you're not too keen on having child number three."

I opened up to Al, and all my fears and concerns came gushing out. "How am I going to pay for the cost of delivery and support this child when I'm already living from hand-to-mouth? What will happen if we have a retarded child? What will we do with him or her since we have to travel and minister on the road?" I continued to pour out everything that I could think of.

Al simply diffused all my preconceived notions and assured me by saying, "God's grace is sufficient for you in all circumstances."

His comforting, Godly counsel helped ease my distress a great deal. But I still felt scared inside, and knew I had to come to grips with that fear. I had to surrender to a situation that was unchangeable! There was no return, and I couldn't pass "GO" or collect $200. It wasn't a simple board game of Monopoly. Instead, it was *FOREVER* and very *REAL*!

The whole thing was crazy. I found myself asking everyone who had more than two children at the camp, "What is it like having more than two children?"–as if another child would make a difference.

All of them told me that it was wonderful and encouraged me. They *even* congratulated me upon hearing the news that Marilyn was expecting! Constantly, I was looking for affirmation that all was going to be well. I needed to *KNOW* that *"..all things work together for good to them that love God, to them who are the called according to His purpose"* (Romans 8:28).

One night, after leading children's church, I went into the main chapel area to find Marilyn and to be sociable with the other adults. I spied a man with several children around him and asked, "Are all those children yours?"

He said, "Yes, all ten of them are mine."

I turned pale and gulped, *"TEN?"*

"Yes!" he responded with a smile as if he were the happiest man on earth. He had a look of satisfaction and pride.

I thought to myself, "He is *definitely* 'touched in the head.'" But I did tell him, "Marilyn and I are expecting our third child."

He then offered, "Having three children is still going up hill, but once you reach five, they are easier to have and to want."

I took his advice as an opportunity to share my concerns about having a third child.

He quickly perceived my fears and said, "Brother, that which is not of faith is sin, and, since you are not walking in faith trusting Christ, you are in sin."

WHAM! His words struck deep and to the point, especially since he was a father of ten children. However, the Lord was being patient with me and was about to serve me the final blow to convince me of my errors in my way of thinking.

About three days after the Mendenhalls had returned to their Portland home, I arose for my early morning prayer walk. We were camped just outside of

Glacier National Park in the beautiful mountains of Northern Montana. The morning air was quite cool. I walked slowly because it was still dark outside. As I worked my way toward Flathead River, I was still carrying into prayer my attitude of, "What am I going to do about having another child?" Since the early morning air was chilly, I decided it would be nice to enjoy a small fire and warm myself. I gathered pieces of dry driftwood that bordered the riverside. I spent considerable time selecting the right size of wood pieces and then assembled them into a position that was befitting a true Royal Ranger. I struck a match, and before long, I had a toasty fire. I extended my hands toward its warmth and began to rub my fingers together while sitting on the comfortable sandy riverside. Hearing the river flow alongside me was very soothing and conducive to prayer.

It was in this setting that I heard the distinct voice of the Lord speak to my spirit saying, "Richard, you have just spent a good portion of your time trying to build a fire. Do you recall in My Word when the disciples went fishing and I was on the shore expecting their return? *'As soon then as they were come to land, they saw a fire of coals there, and fish laid thereon, and bread'* (John 21:9). How do you suppose the fire was prepared? Do you imagine that I, too, had to spend some time gathering wood as you just did and then had to fumble with the used flint and steel to try to strike a fire?"

I scarcely had time to reflect upon the question when the Lord, once again, posed another question. "How do you suppose that the fish roasting on the fire got there? Do you think that, before the disciples got near the shore, I spent time trying My hand at fishing and caught those fish by casting a net for them?"

The Lord was then silent and waited for me to reflect and respond to His questions. I was intrigued by the questions and pondered all aspects of how the Lord may have made the fire and secured the fish. After jostling back and forth in my mind all the possible potentials, I concluded and answered my Almighty God, "Lord, it does not seem, nor is it probable, that You would waste Your time gathering wood and trying to net fish in Your resurrected state since You are so consumed with more important matters."

The Lord replied, "You are exactly right!"

I then said, "Then the only way you could have built the fire and gotten the fish was to speak them into existence from thin air by saying, 'Be there!'"

Again, the Lord indicated to me, "You have surmised the point exactly!"

Once again, I was amazed at the little things one often overlooks when reading God's Word, so I said, "Lord, I am really blessed that You have given me a new understanding this morning. Thank you so very much for revealing this truth to me. You can do anything–You're so amazing!"

Upon revealing this newfound truth, the Lord broke through to my spirit with a gentle, but loving, rebuke that I will never forget as long as I live. He said, "Richard, I want to talk to you about the fear and concern you have about Marilyn having another child, including your foolish notion that the baby may be retarded and that you won't have enough money necessary for his birth. If I, the God of all creation, can create fire and fish from nothing and say, 'Be there!' and then they appear, don't you think that

I can provide all that is necessary for the birth of your child? (And by the way, I chose to create the specific species of fish that appeared.) Why do you doubt My ability? Does not the birth of a child mean more to Me than wood for fire or fish for food? You have been in doubt and unbelief. You have not wanted the child that I have planned and purposed for you and Marilyn to raise for My Kingdom. If you only knew how much I love and desire for husbands and wives to have multitudes of children. If you truly knew how I felt, you would never regret having this child or any other child I may choose to give to you and Marilyn. Mark My words that the day is coming when you will regret not having had more children to share in the glory, joy, and presence of My Kingdom."

I was stunned into silence and was ashamed for being so foolish. I wept and apologized to the Lord. I was completely healed of my obstinate attitude in accepting the birth of my third child. I went back to our motor home and shared with Marilyn all that the Lord had shown me. That evening, during the general assembly service, I sat next to Marilyn and sang praises to our Lord with gladness. Out of the clear blue evening sky, while I was enjoying His presence, the Lord whispered into my inner spirit and said, "I am thy shield and reward." It happened so suddenly and without seemingly any outward reason that my attention was captured. I began to meditate on the words.

The more I meditated on the words, the more I was convinced that they were from the Bible, but I couldn't remember where. After trying as hard as I could to remember, I resorted to using my Bible concordance. It was an especially humbling experience, since I had often boasted that I could locate any verse by memory. I looked up the word "shield" and found that the passage was in Genesis 15:1-4, so I opened my Bible and read:

> *"After these things the word of the LORD came unto Abram in a vision, saying, Fear not, Abram: I am thy shield, and thy exceeding great reward. And Abram said, Lord GOD, what wilt thou give me, seeing I go childless, and the steward of my house is this Eliezer of Damascus? And Abram said, Behold, to me thou hast given no seed: and, lo, one born in my house is mine heir. And, behold, the word of the LORD came unto him, saying, This shall not be thine heir; but he that shall come forth out of thine own bowels shall be thine heir."*

The Lord then whispered to me, just as clear as if someone were sitting next to me, saying, "You will have a son, and he will be the seed of your reward. You are to name him 'Joshua', and I will use him to accomplish great things. I have preordained his birth just as I told Jeremiah, the prophet, long ago. I have planned the birth of every soul even before I formed him or her in the mother's womb. I have also, planned for you and Marilyn to have *this* son. Do you remember back in June while you were in White Sulphur Springs on your prayer walk, when I impressed upon you to read Isaiah 44? You thought I was going to increase the seed and fruit of your ministry to children. But that wasn't what I had in mind. It was My foreknowledge that, on that special night in the church parking lot in Great Falls, Montana, Marilyn would

181

conceive by My power and desire your son. Marilyn is carrying the very child I gave to you that night."

I recalled that I had written down in the margin of my Bible the date the Lord had given me His Word from Isaiah 44. So I turned to the passage, and I was astonished! Sure enough, the margin was marked showing me that the Lord had indeed spoken to me about a seed that morning, which was three weeks *before* the conception of our son.

I had no idea that the seed He was speaking of was the new seed of life He had foreordained for our family. All this was going through my mind during the song service as I sat next to Marilyn. Needless to say, my mind was somewhere else in space and time, and I was totally oblivious to what was going on around me. When the Lord was finished dealing with me, I looked toward Marilyn who was on my left and told her, "The Lord just revealed to me that we are going to have a son and we are to name him 'Joshua.'"

Marilyn smiled at me as if to humor me and said, "That's nice." It didn't bother me a bit. *I knew that I knew, that I knew* what the Lord had told me.

Eight months later, on March 17, 1986, in a birthing center, Marilyn delivered our child. While I stood behind her doing my job as a supportive husband and birthing coach, the doctor looked at me and said, "Hey, don't you want to know whether you have a boy or a girl?"

My answer to him was, "I don't need to know. The Lord already told me eight months ago that it would be boy and we are to name him 'Joshua.'"

With a puzzled look, the doctor said, "You're right—it *is* a boy!"

CHAPTER 36

Turning Points

Up until 1989, my ministry primarily spanned the Pacific Northwest with my speaking at children's crusades and camps and at both Christian and public schools. My desire was to expand our ministry, but I didn't know how. I had purposed in my heart never to solicit funds or write to other ministries seeking an invitation to speak. Therefore, I was left with only one recourse. I had to fall down on my knees and seek God and wait upon Him to open the doors for me. Always, through prayer and reading Scripture, the Lord would reassure me that promotion came from Him. *"Lift not up your horn on high: speak not with a stiff neck. For promotion cometh neither from the east, nor from the west, nor from the south. But God is the judge: he putteth down one, and setteth up another"* (Psalm 75:5-7).

Please don't misunderstand my intentions. I was thoroughly content and blessed to be ministering to children. However, one particular event caused me to have a burden to reach out to the parents of the thousands of children to whom I had been ministering over the years. I had been ministering at a Northern California summer camp set amidst the beautiful Sierra Mountains east of Red Bluff. After one of the morning chapel services, I was just outside the church at a picnic table selling my song tapes to about seven children. I noticed one of the sixth-grade boys was wearing a T-shirt with a logo and a picture on it with the word "Ninja." (This was before the *Ninja Turtle* movie was released.) Curiously, I asked the fellow, "What does 'Ninja' mean?"

He answered, "Oh, Little Bear, Ninja is cool! It's just like karate, but it's a different form of the martial arts." He then demonstrated by kicking the air and letting out a Ninja yell.

Impressed, I asked him, "Do you take classes?"

"No, they're too expensive, but I do get to see the movies. There is *Ninja I* and *Ninja II*. They are really neat, and I learn a lot of the basic movements from them," he said.

"Well then, I'll have to rent the videos sometime since you make them sound so good."

Alarmingly, he said, "Little Bear, you don't want to see those movies. They have scenes of naked girls in them. I don't like that part. I only like the Ninja parts that show Bruce Lee in action."

In shock and grief, I said, "How could you do that? They must be '*R*' rated."

"Yes sir—they are. But my friend's mother rents them and we get to watch them when she is busy doing other things. She doesn't know what's on them."

I replied, "Don't do that! I'm an adult, and I won't even watch something like that! How can you allow yourself to see such destructive movies?"

He hung his head in shame and said, "I can't help liking them even though I know they are bad to see."

I was then inspired to speak out a warning to all the youth standing around the picnic table, "Don't see movies like that ever again or movies like *Poltergeist*!"

They all blurted out, "Oh, we've seen that one." One girl said, "I've seen it three times!"

Recognizing the sixth-grade girl, I said, "Didn't I have you at Bethany Bible Camp last summer, and didn't I warn you, during chapel time, about the dangers of movie viewing?"

In an honest and innocent way, she responded, "Little Bear, I was a well-behaved girl and followed your teachings for about three months, but, after a while, I reverted to my old ways, and I became indifferent to all you had taught me during summer camp." I am sure the children didn't know what I was feeling when I heard that little girl's honest response. I was so sad that I quickly dismissed myself to go on a prayer walk into the woods.

After going about a mile out of camp, I burst into gushing tears with grief and a broken spirit. I cried out to my Father and said, "Father, I am a failure as a minister! If these young people to whom I minister are not being affected by what I am teaching year after year and are reverting to their old ways, then what good use am I?"

Within a short time the Lord spoke to my spirit and said, "The problem isn't with you. It is with their parents. They are not reinforcing the Biblical teachings you are giving to their children."

It was as if a light was turned on. I could see the problem clearly. I prayed and asked my Father in Heaven to begin allowing me to switch the focus of my ministry from children to adults and parents. I began to realize that parents were not living holy and blameless lives before their children. So many Christian parents have the motto, "Do as I say—not as I do." How can they expect their children to turn out useful and suitable for the Lord's work if they don't lead by Godly example? This truth was further impressed upon my heart in a more dramatic way.

I had my reasons as to why I told the children around the picnic table not to see *Poltergeist.* Two months prior, I had turned on a television and, while channel surfing, I felt compelled to stop on a particular channel that was airing a movie. If you're like me and choose usually not to watch television because of certain Godly principles, you can go into shock when you do watch it. This is especially true when you realize how far our nation has fallen into moral decay. Hollywood is a gauge as to what the majority of our society finds acceptable and normal. If that were not true, the movie industry would go out of business. They produce what society demands.

The movie depicted a scene in which a family had gone to sleep while viewing a late night show on television. It appeared that the family, consisting of a father, mother, and two children, fell asleep together in the same bed. As I sat watching, the daughter in the movie, who appeared to be about four years old, woke up and crawled out of bed. While her family was still asleep, she went over to the television. She sat in front of the screen wondering where the picture had gone and why there was only "off the air" static. As the little girl was sitting about one foot in front of the screen, an invisible spirit's hand crept out of the television and possessed her. In a flash second, I turned off the television. I was scared and disturbed in my spirit. I couldn't shake off the experience and the way I was feeling. For several days I was in a quandary and sought the Lord in prayer as to why I was feeling fearful and disturbed. I also wondered what the name of the movie was.

Shortly thereafter, I happened to call a dear friend of mine. His twelve-year-old son answered the phone and, after greeting me, he said, "Little Bear, did you see *Poltergeist* last week? It was really cool."

Now, I knew the name of the movie, but I was disturbed that this Christian boy who came from a committed Christian family had been allowed to see such demonic trash. While I was praying about the reasons as to why I was feeling so bad about the movie, the Lord broke through and revealed to me some startling truths. I pray that I will never forget them and that I will live up to them all the days of my life. Furthermore, I pray that I will teach the Lord's truths to as many people as He will allow me to instruct.

The Lord instructed me by saying, "The feelings you're having are valid."

One particular feeling that I had while watching the movie was that the spirit's hand that had crept out of the television to possess the child was also, literally, coming into the room where I was at the time. The reason I wanted to turn off the television so quickly was that I wanted to stop the manifestation of that spirit from entering into my presence. I questioned the Lord about it, and He revealed to me that was exactly what was happening. I asked Him, "Can a demonic spirit be transferred through television?"

The Lord answered clearly, "Yes." Then He confirmed it with His Word as He directed me to Ephesians 2:1-3: *"And you hath He quickened, who were dead in trespasses and sins; Wherein in time past ye walked according to the course of this world, according to the prince of the power of the air, the spirit that now worketh in the children of disobedience."*

My eyes locked onto the words that read "the power of the air." Immediately, I thought to myself, "Yes, air waves fit well here. The demonic spirits can utilize the air to transfer themselves into the ignorant and foolish viewer's body via the eye gate. Once the demonic spirit has entered, it begins to cause destruction just like what happened to the little girl viewing the television in the movie *Poltergeist.*

Thus, I had my reasons as to why I told the children at camp not to view *Poltergeist* and why I was shocked to hear that so many of them had seen it without any concern or awareness of the dangers. I knew that I had to warn parents, and thus, a new direction for our ministry was birthed. My children's meetings gradually came to a halt and, providentially, the Lord began to open up opportunities for me to teach adults.

One day while we were living in Portland, Oregon, I received a phone call from Sue Welch, the editor of *The Teaching Home* magazine. She told me that *The Teaching Home* was hosting the first national Home School Conference at the Red Lion Hotel in Portland and that her M.C. was unable to fulfill the task. As a result, she asked, "Would you like to be our M.C.?"

To me that was like asking a dog, "Do you like red, juicy meat for dinner?" So, of course, humbly and with great joy, I answered, "Yes."

I was given the opportunity to lead worship and introduce various speakers along with short historical vignettes. During this time of our ministry, I was only slightly known within limited Christian circles in the Pacific Northwest and California. The opportunity that Sue offered me was ordered of the Lord, for it changed the direction of our ministry even to this day.

During the course of the conference, I ministered as M.C. and was able to stand before home school leaders from various states throughout the country. The Lord granted me favor in their sight and, within one year, our ministry expanded and became a national ministry.

"My son, forget not my law; but let thine heart keep my commandments. . . . Let not mercy and truth forsake thee: bind them about thy neck; write them upon the table of thine heart: So shalt thou find favour and good understanding in the sight of God and man. Trust in the LORD . . . and He shall direct thy paths" (Proverbs 3:1-6).

I will forever be grateful to Sue Welch for allowing me the honor to minister at that conference. The Lord allowed me to fulfill my heart's desire, *"Delight thyself also in the LORD; and He shall give thee the desires of thine heart"* (Psalm 37:4). I began ministering to parents by helping them train their children and themselves so that they could fulfill the high calling that God desired for them—all for His glory.

As I began flying out from Portland, Oregon, to as far as the East Coast and experiencing the change of several time zones, it became apparent to me that our ministry base should be better located in a central state. I didn't know where, when, or how a move should come about, but I was willing if God opened the door.

While touring around the country, I was able to take time before and after speaking engagements to visit used bookstores. I began to amass quite a library of rare and out-of-print historical and juvenile books. Considering the fact that I was labeled as being "retarded" and unable to read until I was twelve years old, I think God must have a sense of humor to have given me a great love for books and to use me as a publisher of children's books. In fact, I must confess that I am almost a bibliomaniac. It is a rare "disease" in which one cannot go anywhere without having a book in hand or go shopping without buying a book. If you want to know if you really have a problem, you'll know it for sure when you want to tear down a wall in your home so you can enlarge a room to hold more books. I have all the symptoms.

CHAPTER 37

Book Publishing

My quest for historical non-fiction and juvenile fiction books has proved to be a good thing. I have collected several lost and forgotten books of redemptive value. I found one particular book to be of great interest. It is Governor William Bradford's *History of Plimoth Plantation*. The book tells of how he and the Pilgrim fathers were called of God during the Reformation and their trials and struggles of establishing a beachhead for Christ in America. After reading my particularly cheap out-of-print paperback, I was convinced that I must somehow reprint it. I realized that we, as Americans, have lost the vision of God's original intent when He established our nation.

However, I was faced with a few obstacles. The copy of the book I own was written in ancient out-of-use English, and only a Pilgrim fanatic such as myself would even want to read such a difficult book. All of the *f* letters look like *s* letters. Upon investigation, I discovered that it was going to be an expensive proposition.Where was I going to get the money for printing? Remember we had made a commitment not to ask people for financial support even if it were for projects that would be for their own good. I was over a barrel and, thus, the idea would have to remain a matter of prayer and waiting upon the Lord as to His will and His timing.

As I continued to pray for the Lord to show me a

way to obtain the finances for reprinting, I was tempted many a time to write and ask people on our growing mailing list to help. I was easily able to justify it because the reprinting of valuable rare books would be not for me but for the very people who would be supporting the project. I kept thinking, "Why not seek backers who believe in such a worthy project?"

All my mental wrangling was to no avail as I knew deep down inside that it would be wrong and against the specific command the Lord had given me, "Do not solicit funds for anything whatsoever even if it appears to be for a worthy cause."

In December of 1986, Marilyn and I packed up our motor home and headed out for our annual trip to Pacific Palisades, California. We had plans to minister for about two months and visit with Marilyn's family. Again, we used her parents' driveway as a base station for our RV while we were ministering.

On January 10, around 8:30 p.m., I decided to go on a prayer walk. The walk near my mother-in-law's home is lovely because it is close to the bluffs overlooking the Pacific Coast Highway. On that particular evening, I hadn't walked but about three houses down toward the bluffs when I heard the unmistakable voice of the Lord directing me, "Go back and ask Mr. Cobb to reconsider eternal life."

Mr. Cobb or "Pops," as we endearingly call him, was like a father to me, as I had grown to dearly love him over the years. I always looked forward to visiting with him and Mrs. Cobb. Over the course of my married life, the Lord has placed Robert Cobb on my heart, and I have prayed for him constantly. His greatest fault was that he was vehemently opposed to, what he termed in his typical Scottish accent, "foolishness of religion." He was an avowed atheist and proud of it. Whenever we discussed Christianity, he would bring out a full arsenal and fire retorts against the claims of Christianity, for all he was worth.

During the early days of my walk with Christ, I was foolishly convinced that I could persuade him toward Christianity. However, as I matured, I grew to understand what Christ taught, *"...No man cometh unto the Father, but by Me"* (John 14:6). So, over the years, I talked less and prayed more. There were times that I would fall down upon my knees and weep uncontrollably for his soul. I perceived that the Holy Spirit inspired this kind of prayer. At other times, I would ask others to remember him in prayer. Marilyn once declared a truth when she said, "You pray more for my father than I do."

My response was, "It isn't I, but it is a burden the Lord has asked me to carry."

I carried the burden for over fifteen years. So, when the Lord told me to return from my prayer walk and go back to the house and ask Pops to reconsider eternal life, I obeyed. However, I responded with reservation because I knew it would result in an uncomfortable verbal battle. It would be like a naval engagement firing broadside into each other and, all the while, trying to convince each other of his error.

The impression to go back immediately was so strong that I felt I must not lose a moment of time, so I turned around and went back. Upon entering the house, I found Pops in a perfect setting. He was sitting all alone reading the paper. I took a seat on the opposite side of the couch to brace myself for the battle and then waited for a burst of courage. Just as I was about to share what the Lord had instructed me to, Mrs. Cobb, the peacemaker, walked into the room with Marilyn. I had waited too long to gain courage, and so I lost my opportunity. "Oh well, there will always be another time," I thought to myself. The problem with my rationale was that it became very clear to me the following morning that there may never be another time!

CHAPTER 38

"Richard—Come Quick! Pops Has Fallen!"

Those words, *"Richard—Come Quick! Pops Has Fallen!"* will forever be etched upon my mind. On January 10, 1987, we gave our family and friends a final farewell as we were planning to head back to our Portland home the following morning. We tucked Noelle and Aimee into their bunks and put four-year-old Joshua into his bathtub bed. Our RV was getting a mite too small for a family of five. Mind you, I am not complaining, as I have learned the lesson of Philippians 4:11, *"...I have learned, in whatsoever state I am, therewith to be content."*

Long before 1987, I had learned in a very unique way to be content. I had been rushing about in our twenty-four-foot RV as I was putting on a "Little Bear" outfit for a church meeting. As I walked into the bathroom, my baby toenail caught the edge of the doorframe and was lifted right off. Marilyn and the children had already left and were at the church. I certainly did not have time to lose a toenail, since I had only fifteen minutes before I was scheduled to speak. Generally, I am very calm and collected about personal mishaps. However, this time, especially since we had been on a several-month tour in the crowded RV and the fact that I was in a hurry, I lost my self-control.

I grabbed my toe and while sitting down on the floor I began complaining to God about my situation. Whining, I cried out to God, "Look at me, *Your* son! Why do I have such a small motor home, and how come I have to suffer so much by living in such tight quarters with a family of five? Why can't I have something bigger like a $100,000 Blue Bird coach? You know—as some of those other full-time ministries have. If I had a bigger coach, I would not have stubbed my toe!"

As I lamented over my fate in life and was feeling sorry for myself, I tried to find a bandage. Within moments, the Lord calmly spoke a word to me that I shall remember all the days of my life. He has a way of dispelling every argument we think is justifiable. He said, "The apostle Paul would have loved to have your RV while traveling throughout Asia Minor." My case was closed. I was not only knocked on the point of my toe, but knocked on the point of my head by the Lord.

As I was saying, we were all tucked in bed for the night and soon fell fast asleep. At precisely 3:10 a.m., our eight-year-old Aimee called out to us saying she felt sick. Since I slept on the outside of the over-the-cab bunk bed, I rolled out first to help her to the bathroom. After a minute or two, Marilyn and I tucked her back into bed and then we crawled up into our bunk. At 3:20 a.m., Aimee called out again for help. I told Marilyn just to sleep, as I would take care of things. Once again, I ministered to Aimee and we went back to bed for the second time. Only this time, as I was wide-awake, I asked the Lord to heal Aimee and to comfort her in her affliction. The stomach flu had been spreading amongst the Cobb family during this particular annual visit. As I was in prayer, I heard the sound of what appeared to be someone getting sick inside a house. Our RV was parked between two houses that were typically close for homes in a big city. I figured that it was a male making the sound and that it was either Pops or the neighbor. I turned my prayer attention from Aimee to the sound that I heard and asked the Lord to comfort whoever was sick. Since the flu had been running around, I just figured that perhaps Pops was getting stomach sickness.

Within moments I heard a rap on our RV door and a frantic voice saying, "Richard, come quick! Pops has fallen!"

It was Marilyn's mother. Her call to me struck me like the tone of voice that Jesus used when He called Lazarus from the grave. I was wide awake and dressed in joggers. I was out in a flash, and, just as quickly, the Lord spoke to me saying, "Robert Cobb's soul is required of him this very day."

It immediately dawned on me as to why the Lord had been so emphatic with me, just hours before, to ask Robert if he would re-consider eternal life in Christ Jesus. Instinctively, I recalled the verse which says, *And as it is appointed unto men once to die, but after this the judgment"* (Hebrews 9:27). While I was running to the bathroom where Pops had fallen, the Lord revealed to me that this was His divinely, appointed hour for Robert Cobb. I found Pops stretched out on the floor against the bathtub. I knelt down to get closer to him so I could see if I could help him in any way. He appeared to be already dead. His eyes were glazed over, and his mouth quivered with the last vestiges of life.

I immediately cried out to the Lord, "O, Lord, just give me *one more* opportunity to ask Robert to consider eternal life. I know You instructed me earlier this evening to ask him to reconsider salvation. *Pleeease* just give me *one* more chance!"

Miraculously, right before my eyes, Pops' eyes became crystal clear and he stopped quivering the spasms of death. He focused his eyes upon Marilyn as she and her mother were just entering the bathroom. Faintly, he said, "Marilyn—I feel sick."

Both Marilyn and her mother, Margaret, thought that he meant his stomach was sick, so they ran off to get a container, as it was obvious that he wouldn't be able to move to the toilet. I was grateful for the opportunity to be alone with him. I gently placed my hand underneath his head and began to stroke his head for comfort. The container was delivered and the ladies ran off to call Marilyn's sister so they could tell her about his critical condition. I recalled that he had once warned me, if I ever happened to be by his side when he was dying, not to bother getting a deathbed confession from him. Knowing and remembering his words, I still had to ask him at that precise moment, "Pops, will you consider eternal life?"

With a curse and as bold as he could possibly exhale, he answered, "No!"

I wasn't surprised by his response. He immediately expired. I felt him die in my hands; however, I didn't give up. I continued to supplicate to him that he was bound for hell if he didn't repent and receive Christ Jesus as his Savior. One of my Bible seminary teachers had once told me that he had prayed over a coma victim and, although the person appeared to be dead, he could still hear. When the victim came out of his coma, he remembered hearing Bible verses being read to him. My hope and prayer was that Robert would see demons, angels, or anything in the spirit world and quickly repent while in his last moment of life on earth. God only knows the outcome of his soul.

I canceled a couple of meetings so I could help officiate at the funeral. Robert died at age seventy-nine. He had survived working in a war factory during World War II and diligently doing hard labor the rest of his life. He was a typical frugal Scotsman who scrimped and saved every penny. He left his inheritance to his wife and three children.

After the legal documents were executed, we returned to our home in Oregon with Marilyn's inheritance. I had never seen so much money in my entire life! The Lord had tested me year after year with trials in which I never knew where our next meal would come from or how I was going to pay the mortgage payment and maintain a home. Yet, I stuck to my guns and never sent "beg letters" to coerce people into supporting our ministry. The Lord was faithful to reward my diligent trust in Him alone and, amazingly, blessed me beyond my prayers and expectations. After tithing on the inheritance money, we paid off our mortgage. This was the mortgage that the Lord had assured me would be paid off within five years. It was actually paid off within three years! We also bought another home for my mother.

I have never thought much of money or had much interest in acquiring large sums of it. Thus, in a very short while, we spent all but about $30,000 of it. For years, I had dreamed of owning a 1962 Corvette, and Marilyn was good-natured enough to leave the remaining portion of her inheritance in my hands to dispose of however I wanted. The decision seemed easy, of course, since I wanted a Corvette and the timing seemed perfect. I began looking in the trade papers for my dream car.

One day, while I was looking through the papers, I heard the voice of the Lord ask me, "Richard, what are you doing?"

"I'm looking for a Corvette. Do *You* know where one is?"

In my spirit, He answered, "Yes, I know where there are lots of Corvettes, but I want to talk to you about publishing books with the money you have remaining."

I acted sort of stupid and said, "What books?"

In a somewhat humorous way, the Lord said, "Don't play dumb with Me. You know perfectly well *what* books I am talking about. Remember the books that you have been praying about republishing for the past several years? I have now answered your prayer, so instead of using the money to buy a Corvette, use it to republish the books."

That wasn't exactly what I wanted to hear. I had hoped, instead, that the Lord would lead me to a Corvette. But I knew He was right and that I needed to use the money to publish the books. I had enough money to print William Bradford's *A History of Plimoth Plantation* and *A Cloud of Witnesses* by Stephen Northrop. Thus, I surrendered to the Lord's will and committed to being, in my mind, a big fool and blow all the money to reprint the two titles.

First, to my way of thinking, my problem was that I didn't know where I was going to store a total of six thousand books in my house. Secondly, I didn't know how the word would get out to people to know that the books were for sale since I was a small-time "unknown" evangelist. After all, I had never been on Dr. Dobson's or Dr. James Kennedy's radio program, and if one hasn't been on either program then he or she is considered a "nobody" in mainstream Christianity.

All I can say is that I obeyed and trusted God. Now as I look back over the many years, the Lord has been ever faithful as we have published sixty-two titles and sold many thousands of books since 1988. We have received many letters throughout the years from people who just wanted to thank us for republishing books that have been heart-warming and encouraging to them and their family. Owning a Corvette could never have accomplished the eternal value of serving the Lord by making those books available, that were written by precious authors who were anointed by God and who wrote for His glory. One of my greatest joys and sense of satisfaction will be to meet the authors of the books that I have republished in their honor when we meet in eternity before the throne of our King Jesus. Can you imagine Martha Finley coming up to me with amazement that someone had actually taken her *Elsie Dinsmore* and *Mildred Keith* books and republished them over one hundred years after she had gone on to her eternal reward? Just think, even though many years have passed, those lost and forgotten books still have the power to lead the young and the old alike to know and grow in the Lord Jesus Christ and to cause them to love and serve Him.

CHAPTER 39

Texas or Bust!

As I sought the Lord in my daily devotions, He continued to impress upon me that He would guide and provide for my family. He made it clear that if I put Him first in my life, He would take care of us and direct our steps. For several years, I tried to video record our ministry, so, in my attempt, I bought expensive equipment and hired production companies.

At every turn, each of my attempts to record our ministry on video led to failure. After a while, I became so frustrated that I simply lost the desire to proceed any further. My goal was to have captured, on video, some of the historical stories that the Lord had given me. I wanted to preserve them for my children along with my historical devotional audio cassettes. Since I felt that it was important to leave a legacy to my children of what God did, from a Christian and providential perspective, to establish this nation, video recordings were an important element that I didn't want to overlook.

Providentially, during the season of wanting to video record, I received a call from Cecelia Leininger, a Christian mother in San Antonio, Texas. She had called to inquire as to where I would be ministering during the upcoming summer months. I told her what my schedule was to be and that I was very sorry, but I didn't have any plans to be in Texas. I had never ministered in Texas and couldn't foresee doing so, anytime, in the near future. I had to tell her that I wasn't even going to be anywhere near Texas so that her family could attend one of my meetings.

Cecelia proceeded to tell me that her family loved my historical devotional cassette stories. I was humbled to hear such news and blessed that someone would call all the way from Texas to tell me that she desired to see and hear my ministry in person. She continued to say that her husband, Jim, had recently been playing the historical tapes in their car cassette player. While listening to the tapes on their return trip home, the children were sitting in the back seat "quiet as church mice" listening intently. When Jim pulled into their driveway and turned off the car engine, all three of the children, in unison, said, "Wait, Dad—we haven't heard the rest of the story yet!" They were so adamant that Jim turned the ignition back on so they could finish hearing the story. It was then that he realized that he had to purchase the entire set of tapes for the children because it was rare for anyone to be able to captivate them in such a fashion.

Once again, I thanked Cecelia for the account, and asked her family to remember me in their prayers. She then asked me about my Montana summer ministry, which I had told her about in passing. She told me that it might be possible for them, as a family, to fly to Montana to meet me and my family. She thought it would be wonderful for her children to actually see the face of the voice that had grown familiar to them. I thought, "Surely, my own mother wouldn't come that far to hear me or see me minister—I doubt that this woman and her family will." Nevertheless, I was polite and gave her the name and phone number of the woman to contact who was the camp coordinator so they could make arrangements just in case they decided to go.

Summer came soon enough, and we found ourselves submerged in ministry at children's camps throughout Montana. For the third consecutive summer, we returned to Hungry Horse to minister. About midweek, after morning chapel, a family of five came up and introduced themselves as the Leininger family. I couldn't believe it! They came all the way from Texas to meet us just because my devotional cassette stories had ministered to their children.

Now, looking back over the many years past, I can honestly say that I believe friendships are made in Heaven, which was definitely the case with the Leininger family. At the time, they had three children—Brian, Kelly, and Tracy. Later Joshua came as a special gift of the Lord. Our children hit it off like bread and jam. We hated to see them part from our lives when they left only four days later. We discovered that our families shared many of the same Biblical convictions. This has always been very important to us, and we are cautious as to whom we allow our children to have as friends. It is always a blessing to share a friendship with parents who are like-minded.

At the end of that summer, we returned to Portland at which time I was invited to minister at the National Home School Conference the following spring. During the conference, lo and behold, the Leiningers, once again, showed up and our friendship was renewed. Keep in mind that I had been praying off and on about the video recordings. I kept reminding the Lord that I was waiting for Him to open the door and that I wouldn't move into this area of desire without His certain help and direction.

Six months later, I was invited to minister at a small Christian school in Banks, Oregon, which was about forty minutes west of Portland. I had ministered there for about three years, leading the chapel service. After chapel, the principal asked me if I had ever considered putting my messages on video. I snickered and told her that I had, and, in fact, I had even attempted to do so; however, I had been a complete failure in my attempts to record them in my own strength. I asked her to pray about the project because I was willing if the Lord was willing. The very next morning, Dr. Jim Leininger called me and revealed to me that he had purchased a small local television station. He wanted to know if I would be willing to come down to San Antonio, Texas, to tape a Christmas program. As you can imagine, I was most excited and delighted at the prospect.

CHAPTER 40

Remember the Alamo

I immediately liked Texas and Texans, and I could understand why my childhood hero, Davy Crockett, had come to Texas. I videotaped the Christmas special and met many new homeschool families who embraced me with loving kindness—the Boone, Sheeran, Miller, Sanford, Staffel, and Harris families are only a few to mention. My return home was one of life's bittersweet experiences. It was sweet because I was returning home to my family and friends, but it was bitter because I had to leave a part of my heart back in San Antonio. Being able to video record in a real live studio with real cameras that worked was wonderful! While on the return flight home, I prayed and dreamed of someday being able to move to Texas. I didn't realize that the Lord was already setting the stage.

Jim and Cecelia invited me to return to San Antonio the following spring to speak at their annual citywide track and field event. Once again, I felt a tug in my spirit to move to Texas. Our ministry had begun to expand since I had spoken at the First National Homeschool Conference in Portland which had exposed my gifts and calling to homeschool leaders. God gave me favor in their sight, and I began to receive bookings as a keynote speaker at homeschool events from the West Coast to the East Coast. I will always be grateful to the pioneers of the homeschool movement and the leaders who gave me the opportunity to minister in their states. As a result of our ministry expanding, it became evident that a move to Texas would make traveling through various time zones much more appealing.

Again, I left Texas and returned home to consult with Marilyn about making a major move after having lived in Oregon for twelve years. We both could see the wisdom in such a decision. Additionally, we found that our prayerful desire to videotape my messages was being answered. In fact, Jim Leininger told us that he would make his camera crew available to me for video taping our messages, and that they would edit all of the videos at no cost to us. As God seemed to have been guiding and providing, we decided to sell our home. We figured that the Lord would send us a buyer if He wanted us to move. Within three weeks, we sold our house and were off to San Antonio, where we found ourselves house-hunting again.

We found a home in a subdivision we liked and made an offer, which was accepted, but reluctantly so. I say reluctantly because I learned later from the cheerful wife that the husband did not want to sell the home; however, his wife did. The wife had won an argument. The husband placed the home on the market on only one condition: that the house would be on the market for only one week, and if it didn't sell by then, he would pull it back off. He told the wife that if she didn't like that condition then it was just too bad for her.

We arrived in San Antonio on a Sunday and contacted our Christian realtors, Adrian and Gloria Arbuzo, who are now dear friends of ours. We made arrangements to start house-hunting the next Monday morning. We checked all the computer listings of houses on the market in Hollywood Park that were within our price range. Monday and Tuesday proved to be fruitless; nothing was to our liking. However, on Wednesday morning, I told Marilyn that I was going to have a look around by myself while she waited at the Leiningers' for Adrian and Gloria. I hadn't been gone for more than twenty minutes when I spotted a house that we hadn't noticed before. I wrote down the listing agent's phone number and reported my find to our agents. It seemed that the house had just been placed on the market on Monday (just two days earlier), so it wasn't listed in the computer yet. Therefore, our agents hadn't had access to the information. Nevertheless, we made arrangements to see the house. Immediately, we both knew that it was the home for us. When the owner heard that an offer had been made only three days into the seven to which he had agreed, he was shocked. Since he had made the agreement with his wife, he was over a barrel and had no choice but to sell the home to us. We knew it was a sign from the Lord and a confirmation that we were in His will in moving to San Antonio.

CHAPTER 41

Time of Growth

I never cease to be amazed when it comes to the Lord's timing. A person can earnestly pray for many years to see the fulfillment of a dream. Then, in just a moment of time, the Lord can accomplish what took years of desire and prayer. Moving to San Antonio was a blessing in so many ways. It just so happened that our house was only three blocks away from the TV station. Our ministry was growing at a healthy rate. However, during our first few years of living in San Antonio, I was not booked to speak as heavily as in later years. The Lord fulfilled my dream and desire by giving me more time on my hands along with the generosity of Jim's offer to videotape my messages. It is not likely I could have ever afforded to tape and edit even two or three videos—let alone the fourteen videos that we have done to date. God indeed is an awesome God.

Another totally unexpected blessing was when my dear friend Dr. Jim Leininger asked me if I wanted to hunt at his hunting lease. I asked him, "When is hunting season, and what is a hunting lease?" He told me that the deer-hunting season in Texas was during the month of December and extended into early January. I couldn't believe what I heard! Being an evangelist, I didn't have meetings in December because most churches were gearing up for Christmas programs; therefore, I had the entire month off.

Jim told me that, unlike most other states, the majority of hunting in Texas was done on privately owned land. Being able to hunt meant paying a landowner a large sum of money for permission to hunt on his property. I later read that it cost an average of three hundred dollars to shoot a deer in Texas. I don't know about anyone else, but I don't like venison enough to pay three hundred dollars for approximately sixty pounds of lean meat. I figure for that kind of money a person could buy a lot more beef. I told Jim, "Thank you, but I can't afford to pay to hunt. In fact, I put aside my rifle many years ago while living in Oregon, and so I have become content not to hunt."

Rather chagrined, Jim told me, "I am not asking you to pay—you can hunt on my lease for free." I was elated! I did not have a decent rifle, so I went out and purchased a used rifle and secured a hunting license, which made me a proud "bona fide" Texas hunter.

Hunting in Texas doesn't seem very sportsman-like to me. A hunter places corn out on a dirt road. Then he climbs up a fifteen-foot hunting blind tower and sits in a swivel chair looking out over a 360° view. The hunter remains there in waiting until a group of deer smells the corn and then comes to the road to eat it. The hunter sizes up the deer, choosing the best of the bunch, and then shoots it. He climbs back down the hunting blind, goes to his truck, backs it up to the deer where he muscles the critter into the back of the truck, and then drives it to a cabin where he will skin and hang it.

The ultimate goal, however, is to be able to shoot a "monster" buck that is out there *somewhere*. I like to be more practical and adventurous. I would much rather sit on the ground in the midst of danger where I could get attacked by a crazy wild hog, or bitten by a rattlesnake. It makes it much more challenging.

After my first hunting season in Texas, I was very grateful to Jim and the Lord for allowing me the opportunity to enjoy being outdoors amongst God's creation again and pray. Generally, I have almost always hunted for the meat and not just for sport. We have lived off deer meat for several years, and have found it to be very healthful especially in comparison to the fat content of store-bought beef. After giving up hunting in exchange for more time to evangelize while living back in Oregon, I never could have imagined being able to get the opportunity to hunt again. It is just like the Lord to bless us more than we bless Him. If we follow and obey Him, He will always out-give us. One can never out-give the Lord, which is a truth I have discovered during my Christian life. *"Give, and it shall be given unto you; good measure, pressed down, and shaken together, and running over, shall men give into your bosom. For with the same measure that ye mete withal it shall be measured to you again"* (Luke 6:38).

CHAPTER 42

Giving Back to the Lord His Due

Writing this portion of my biography is difficult. I realize that the reader may misunderstand my heart and purpose and think that I am boasting. However, I must write this chapter so that I may encourage my own children whom the Lord has given to Marilyn and me as well as encourage the reader of this book. The subject of giving is such a personal and private matter that most people do not generally like to discuss it. Yet, the Bible is full of teachings on "giving." In fact, the greatest teacher on the subject of "giving" is the Giver of Life Himself—Jesus Christ. God is the greatest Giver of all. We know this by examining what He did for all mankind, *"For God so loved the world, that He gave His only begotten Son, that whosoever believeth in Him should not perish, but have everlasting life"* (John 3:16). The old adage that "no one can out-give God" is so true. The truth is evidenced by the fact that Jesus gave His life for those He loved even while those He loved didn't love Him. *"Greater love hath no man than this, that a man lay down his life for his friends"* (John 15:13). And so, we love and give because He *"...first loved us"* (I John 4:19).

Sad to say, it appears that the majority of Christians are not even trying to obey and prove God in the area of tithing and giving. Statistics show that Christians, as a whole, do not give tithes to the work of the Lord. It has been reported that if every Christian would give his tithe to his local church, churches would never need to assume any debt. Actually, there would be more than enough money to meet the needs of the people in the church and outside of the church. What a testimony the Church would have if we would only be obedient.

When Christians stop giving, the government fills the void, which results in the people losing the proper perspective that God is our provider. Sadly, as a result, unbelievers and immature Christians expect the government to supply all their needs. Ironically, the people are still dependent on God for His provision, as it is He who gives man the ability to work and earn a living. Then because of our disobedience we are *forced* to pay taxes that become a greater burden than even our God would require. We put ourselves in bondage. Disobedience leads to deception, and God's people are deceived into thinking that it is the *government* who is the provider. They remain blind to the fact that the government *demands* and *takes* 30 percent or more of their income. Then the government uses the money that we are forced to give for whatever purposes they deem appropriate, whether for noble or wicked works. Bureaucratic leaders get rich by the sweat of our brow and all because we haven't loved God with our whole heart and obeyed His Word.

God requires only 10 percent of what He gave to us in the first place. He owns everything and is so gracious to give His people 90 percent of what is His. Yet we begrudge Him of the 10 percent He asks of us. Could you imagine what life in America would be like if we obeyed God with tithing? We could give the Lord 20 percent of our income, and we would still have less of a burden than we now have to endure. We would be able to give to whomever and wherever the Lord led us. What a blessing that would be! Oh, but we are such a stubborn generation that we have cursed ourselves and serve a government that will continue to increase our taxes and place us under a heavier burden.

> "Ye are cursed with a curse: for ye have robbed me. . . . Bring ye all the tithes into the storehouse, that there may be meat in mine house, and prove me now herewith . . . if I will not open you the windows of heaven, and pour you out a blessing, that there shall not be room enough to receive it. And I will rebuke the devourer for your sakes . . . all nations shall call you blessed . . . saith the Lord of hosts" (Malachi 3:9-12).

Because Christians do not choose to govern themselves (being directed by and submitting to the Holy Spirit) we lose sight of the fact that *we* are providing for ourselves out of the provision that *God* has given to each of us. Furthermore, the Bride of Christ loses her blessing and opportunity to demonstrate her Bridegroom's power and ability to provide. It is absurd when Christians stop giving to the work of the Lord and then have the audacity to praise the government for meeting their needs. This grieves my heart because it is God Almighty alone who is worthy to receive glory and honor. When the government receives the glory, God's heart is broken as He is just waiting to be proved so that He can bless His people with abundance. When Jesus is not Lord of our finances, our works become dead and we do not manifest the reality that we are serving a *living* God. The heart-wrenching part is that those who desperately need to know our King Jesus and His government remain lost. We have lost souls for Him because our testimony has become diminished.

Immediately after our salvation experience, Marilyn and I attended an evening Bible study at a fellow believer's home in West Los Angeles. That particular night, the leader chose a topic regarding *"tithing to the Lord on all that comes across your hands."* We received the message into our hearts hook, line, and sinker. The combination of that message and the message on "giving" that Pete gave to me (whom I believe was an "angel unaware") caused me to accept without hesitation the practice of tithing 10 percent of any income I would ever receive.

Over the years, we have found that tithing and giving should not depend on an attitude of "only give when you can afford it." Instead, one should give to the Lord *first* even if it doesn't appear possible to still make ends meet. Because we have made a steadfast commitment to give to the Lord, I believe that He has been faithful and has blessed us in untold measure. *"Give, and it shall be given unto you; good measure, pressed down, and shaken together, and running over, shall men give into your bosom. For with the same measure that ye mete withal it shall be measured to you again"* (Luke 6:38).

However, I must confess that it has not always been easy to hold onto the principle of tithing. There were many times when we had so little money that we did not know where our next meal would come from, but the Lord always provided. Oftentimes, Christians assume that, someday, when they get enough money they will have

215

plenty to give and it will not be as painful to part with. I find this kind of rationale to be deceiving because one can always justify that he does not have enough money to give at any particular time. There never seems to be enough money to satisfy our sinful desires and selfish natures. Over the course of our Christian walk, I have found that, as we are faithful in giving to the Lord, He always gives more back to us—even to the point of giving us more than enough to meet our needs. Many times, He even gives us our desires.

After reading accounts of great men of God, such as George Muller and J. C. Penney, who gave much more than just a tithe in their lifetimes, I became inspired to give more each year above my tithe. This has been quite scary, to tell the truth. Consider the reality of such a step of seemly blind faith. For example, if you normally tithe $250 each month, you would double it the following year to $500 per month. I exhort you to start increasing your tithe, so you will experience this blessing from God. You will begin to appreciate and comprehend what I mean when I tell you that it is scary to give in abundance, but you will also begin to see God's blessings pour out upon you without measure.

By faith, I increased my tithe to 25 percent for one year. I increased my tithe by 5 percent each following year. I am not sure when to stop, but I will travel this road until the Lord shows me otherwise. It has been exciting, to say the least. The most astounding thing about it all is that I haven't seen the bottom of the bucket yet! It has been like the widow in Elijah's day whose wheat barrel never went empty even though she gave all of what little she had to the prophet of God. (See I Kings 17:8-16.)

Let me tell you a story about the truth on tithing and giving that became imbedded in me, to the core of my being. The Lord prompted me, some time ago, to give a generous sum of money to a family in our home church was in desperate need. The sum was much greater than my tithe amount. Initially, I promptly responded to the Lord, wrote out the checks and placed it in my out-going mail bin. The next day the devil's emissaries whispered into my ear and told me that I had given too much and that I had better stop giving beyond my tithe. They continued to tempt me with the thought that I needed to take back a portion of the money and put it into our savings account and that, if I didn't, we wouldn't have enough money to live on whenever we found the need to retire. The temptation was fierce. Each time I walked passed my mail bin, I was tempted to take back the check and rewrite one for half the amount. I struggled for several days, as my Mantle Ministries mail is picked up only twice a week. I resisted each temptation, but I must admit that I was very relieved when the postal truck finally picked up my mail and, with it, my temptation! As the mail truck drove away, I thought, "Oh, well, we have been dirt poor before, and the Lord has always sustained us. Surely, He will take care of us in our retirement years." I also brought to memory the verse "*I have been young, and now am old; yet have I not seen the righteous forsaken, nor His seed begging bread*" (Psalm 37:25).

The following Sunday, our pastor, Peter Spencer, gave a sermon from the Old Testament on the principles of giving and used the examples of Abraham, Isaac, Jacob, and other patriarchs. As he was preaching, one of the principles fell like a gem upon my attentive ears, and I trust that I will never forget it. Pastor Peter said, "Giving to God opens a window for God to give back to the giver. If we stop giving to God, we will rob ourselves of the blessings that God wants to bestow upon us."

The statement wasn't particularly a new revelation to me, since I was very familiar with the passage in Malachi 3:10. However, it was just one of those times when a thought or Scripture leaps out and grabs my heart with just the right words for the right occasion.

At that moment, the Lord spoke to my heart in the following manner and said, "It was a good thing that you did not give into your temptation to remove that check from the mail bin last week and change the amount from what I had prompted you to give to the couple in this church. If you had removed the check and cut another one for a lesser amount, you would have limited Me from ever trusting you with more money. I want to be able to trust you to give money to those to whom I prompt you to give. By giving into your temptation, you would have sealed the limit that I would give to you by the amount for which you would have rewritten the check."

I was dumbfounded and gripped with awe at the responsibility and the far-reaching consequences that were attached to what I thought was a minor temptation. Of course, I was overjoyed that I had passed the test. It was wonderful to know that God could trust me with a financial increase. By Wednesday of that same week, I went to my mailbox and noticed that I had received a royalty check. When I opened the envelope, I found a check that was *TEN TIMES* more than the gift I had given to the young couple! In fact, it was the largest check that I had ever received in twenty years! The Lord demonstrated to me that if I continue to give in abundance, He could and would trust me with more so that I could continue to give to others.

By way of postscript, one of my favorite stories is *A Christmas Story* by Charles Dickens. It is a wonderful reminder that we should be living in a spirit of giving year round. The story always serves to check my spirit as to whether or not I am becoming a "scrooge" in regard to blessing others, which is a good reminder that we all need regularly.

CHAPTER 43

The Life of this Evangelist

As I have already mentioned, we decided, in the first several years of our ministry, to call ourselves "American Heritage Ministries" because we were recapturing the heritage of America's past. But when I applied for a registered legal trade name, I was told that the name was already taken. Therefore, I had no other choice but to pray and seek God for another name for our ministry.

One day as we were pondering what to name our ministry, I told Marilyn that I would like it to have a name that would represent recapturing America's Christian history and, also, express that we had a God-given responsibility to continue passing on our heritage of self-government, which is a foundational stone that our forefathers have laid. That did it! Immediately, Marilyn said, "Mantle Ministries says it all!"

We used Psalm 78:2-3 for our text: "*I will open my mouth in a parable: I will utter dark sayings of old: Which we have heard and known, and our fathers have told us.*"

My desire, then as it is now, is to help families prepare for the coming of the Lord and that they will teach their children to teach their children to be ready for His imminent return. At the same time, I want to defend America's Christian Heritage that is so ignorantly lost.

I suppose that, as most every ministry grows and develops, it is faced with wanting to be accepted as a bona fide legal ministry wherein the government approves its legal status known as a 501c(3). This type of governmental approval entitles a ministry to perform many functions such as fund raising and issuing a tax-exempt receipt to those who make donations so that they can receive a tax deduction on their annual tax return. For many ministries this also represents a considerable relief of tax liability.

I considered applying for this tax exemption and filled out the huge paper trail that was required to obtain the United States government's stamp of approval. I could definitely see the many wonderful benefits it would allow, but I felt a check in my spirit, so I did not submit the paperwork.

Obtaining a government-approved tax-exempt status requires that a ministry not support or promote anything in a political manner. What occurred to me was, "Why, as a minister, would I want to receive the blessing of a government that could control what I would say regarding politics? Besides, wasn't I ultimately accountable to God for what I endorsed and wasn't He my true source of provision? We had purposed not to solicit funds for support so we did not need to be concerned with issuing receipts to those who gave to us. The support for our ministry was left up to God Himself."

Now that I look back over the years, I believe we made a wise decision. I am at peace with the fact that I *"owe no man any thing"* but love (Romans 13:8). I have the freedom to speak without the threat of authorities removing my tax exempt status. I can't imagine that Jesus and His disciples, even in our day and age, would apply for the government's approval to be recognized as a bona fide ministry. Please know that I am not condemning those ministries that have taken this course. I only want to relate to you our convictions and how our ministry operates.

CHAPTER 44

The End of the Trail

One of my favorite Scriptures is *"Therefore, I say unto you, whatever things ye desire, when ye pray, believe that ye receive them, and ye shall have them"*(Mark 11:24). For several years I had the desire to meet Andy Williams and Fess Parker. Somehow, someway, I believed the Lord would bring to pass my desire to meet these two men who have had a great impact on my life, so I could tell them personally how the Lord used them to help steer the course of my life. All I had been able to do for years is pray for the opportunity to meet them, and leave the rest to the Lord for the fulfilment of this desire.

During the thirty-five years of waiting, I would often pray, very earnestly and unceasingly, for their salvation and for the Lord to reveal Himself to them. I recall numerous occasions awakening at three in the morning, burdened to pray for them. It was as if the Lord was giving me a special bond to these two men. The Lord gave me, on several occasions, dreams of Andy Williams that continued to motivate me to intercession.

On May 18-19, 1996, I was scheduled to minister in Springfield, Missouri. I had learned that Andy Williams opened a theater in Branson, so I decided to take Marilyn with me and spend an extra day planning to see the Andy Williams show at his Moon River Theater. I called several months ahead and reserved tickets on May 20, 1996 for the 3:00 PM show. After I reserved the seats, I was inspired to write Mr Williams a short letter, telling him that for thirty five years I had been following his career, for over twenty years I had been praying for him, and that I would like to have the privilege of meeting him either before or after the show. I realized that most performers do not like to be pestered by people and that my chances were slim, but I also knew that with God all thing were possible to him who believes. I committed this to the Lord and went on with my daily ministry. About a month before I was scheduled to head for Missouri, I received an unexpected call from Andy William's secretary, Leslie, saying that Andy would be willing to see us after the show. I thanked her and the Lord, and began to anticipate meeting Mr. Williams.

The show was great and the theater beautifully designed; however, my real desire was to meet Andy. After the show an usher proceeded to our seats and told us to follow her. She took us back stage and knocked on Mr. William's door. He said, "Come in," and we were presented to him. I knew his time was valuable, so after introducing Marilyn, I went right to the point, and told him how the Lord had used him, unknowingly, many years ago when I was just a young teenage boy. I let it be known that he inspired me to pursue a singing profession and to strive to make something of my life. I told him that when kids in Jr.; high and highschool were promiscuous and taking drugs, that I refused to join them because I wanted to be like him, my hero. Then I told him I became a Christian, and I realized how the Lord had used him to help me through the turbulent American years of the 1960s and 70s. I concluded by saying that it was amazing how the Lord was using him in a unique way, even though he didn't realize it then, to influence a boy, who would someday grow up and travel all over America and share the Gospel of Christ to thousands.

I could see that he was overwhelmed and speechless. I then gave him a copy of my republished book *Gaining Favor with God and Man*, shook his hand in thanksgiving, and left. I asked the usher, on the way out of the theater, if it was customary to be able to visit with Andy after the show. She said it was very unusual for this to happen. I then knew it was the Lord that made this possible. The Lord fulfilled one of my desires, but I still had one left. How in the world would I ever meet Fess Parker?

On October 10, 1997, I was scheduled to fly to minister in Santa Barbara, California. I was picked up by my weekend host driver, Eric Helmick. He took me to my meeting place for the Friday night service. I presented a message that included how Davy Crockett—Fess Parker was my childhood hero, and how the Lord used him to inspire me in the early years of my life, when I had such a poor self image.

As I knelt by the bedside for my prayers that evening, the Lord spoke a word to my heart and said, "Would you like to meet Fess Parker?" I said, "You know, Lord, how I would." He then said he would arrange it for me. I calmly went to sleep, fully expecting Him to perform His word to me. The next morning I asked my host family if they knew Fess Parker, and they said they had casually met him at a Republican rally and that he lived in the area. I told them I had always hoped and prayed to meet him. As it turned out, they had a mutual friend who was well acquainted with Fess Parker, so they called her to see if she could make arrangements for me to meet him. I got my hopes up, but they were quickly dashed as they returned to say that the lady who could make the arrangements was out of town. The Lord whispered in my spirit not to lose hope.

I began my Saturday seminar and after releasing everyone for lunch, my host Eric told me that someone who heard me speak the night before personally knew Fess Parker. She could arrange for me to meet him. Eric told me that he had made arrangements for me to visit with Fess on Sunday at 10:00 AM, but that Mr. Parker only had a small amount of time to meet with me because he was going to church to hear a friend sing at 11:00 AM. What is really amazing is when I booked this series of meetings a year earlier, I was told that I would not be able to do the sermon but only teach a Sunday school class. At the time of the booking I thought this unusual, for I generally do the Sunday morning pulpit message whenever I come to an area. However, I was willing to serve in any capacity that was best suited for the church. Little did I know then, that the Lord was going to answer years of prayer. If I had been scheduled to preach the Sunday morning sermon, I would not have been able to meet with Fess Parker.

Eric and I drove to Fess Parker's business in the mountains of Santa Barbara. Fess drove up at the same time and we greeted each other. He was very cordial and invited us to come sit on the patio and chat a while. I told him much of what I had told Andy Williams, and after having heard what role he had played in my early childhood years, humbly said it was not him, but the Lord. I asked him if he was a born-again Christian, and he said, "You had better believe it." I told him I was so glad because I wanted to be his friend in heaven someday. He smiled in a wonderful warm way. We talked for some time, then he said he had to go to church. I asked him if I could pray for him, and he consented. After the prayer, he was teary eyed and touched by the Lord.

Well, the Lord, after many years of labor and prayer, had fulfilled my desire to be able to thank these two men. I have always been a stickler for giving credit where credit is due, and I was obsessed in somehow trying to reach them, but how, was far beyond me. Only the Lord could have made those arrangements. With this dream fulfilled, I now rest in peace and commit them to the Lord through prayer.

CHAPTER 45

It's a Wonderful Life

As part of our annual Christmas tradition in the past, we have always watched *It's a Wonderful Life,* starring Jimmy Stewart and Donna Reed, which like all pictures may have some short comings as we drew nearer to Christ's standards. However, for the sake of example, it is one of our most beloved movies. Scarcely a person living today can watch this movie without experiencing delight and awe at what one person's life can accomplish realizing the impact it may have on others around him.

For some divine reason, ordained by God in His plan and purpose for me, I have as far back as I can remember felt that I have a mission and a purpose in life. That purpose and mission is to serve and love God and all those over whom He grants me the privilege to have some influence. I was one of those kids who took life seriously while growing up and felt that I was accountable to God for my actions or lack thereof. Thus, I was naturally inclined toward service and ministry. I truly wanted to devote my life to His service and will.

I feel that I have been fully rewarded for being an associate pastor, a youth pastor, and now an evangelist. As I look back over my life, I can see how all the paths through which the Lord has led me have been to prepare me for the life of an evangelist.

Often people ask me, "What is it like being an evangelist?"

From my perspective my life is somewhat lonely. That may appear to be strange, since I am around multitudes of people all the time. However, after a meeting when everything is said and done and they all go back to their homes, I often wonder, "Will they remember me and the message I gave to them? Did I plant any seeds that will enable them to grow in the Lord and produce everlasting fruit?"

I have only to hope and trust that, like George Bailey did in the movie, *It's a Wonderful Life,* someday I will know what the Lord accomplished through me and Mantle Ministries. George Bailey had no idea what an impression and to what extent his life touched others until the end of the movie. To himself, he was just an ordinary man doing the mundane things of everyday life. I can often relate to George, and I am sure that many of you can also. Many times being an evangelist can be discouraging, and I become insecure. As a matter of fact, I wrestle with feelings of concern that the Lord will reject me and stop giving me opportunities to minister.

I recall one specific time when I cried out to the Lord in prayer to please not set me aside. I pleaded with Him to continue to open doors for me to minister. He replied to my spirit by saying, "Why would I not continue to use you to minister on My behalf? I am constantly searching for believers to labor for My Kingdom. If I want more people to minister, why would I retire the few that I now have?"

I was relieved and felt a tremendous encouragement to continue ministering without fear of being rejected. Now, whenever I feel insecure, I remember those words and I am encouraged in the Lord.

I want to share with you that I am very grateful to the people who write to me to express their satisfaction and how the Lord has used Mantle Ministries to bless their lives and help them to grow in Christ through my speaking, and producing books, tapes, and videos. Many people have come up to me after listening to me minister for many years just to tell me their testimony of how God used Mantle Ministries to change their lives for the better. Their words are timeless to me and encourage me greatly. I recommend that you give kind and encouraging words to your pastor and to those who impart the Word of God to you.

Following are some encouraging letters that have come to us. They are like manna from Heaven that the Lord has sent to uplift us. They are from the same types of people that George Bailey had show up at the end of the movie in *It's a Wonderful Life.* May God bless all of you who have written and the small bunch of you who have sent us love gifts ever so faithfully over the years.

Dear Little Bear,

I attended the March 8-9, 1996 Gwinnett Christian Home Educators conference (Atlanta, Georgia) where you spoke Friday night and all day Saturday on "America's Godly Heritage." History has never been exciting to me, but hearing of God's movements to accomplish His purposes throughout history fascinated me. I was overwhelmed with what I heard and what God was saying to me through you. I was convicted about how lightly I had treated God's Word. The conference ended abruptly due to time constraints ,and so I walked away stunned—not knowing what to do with all of it. I wished there could have been an altar call. I just wanted you to know that your ministry has changed my life. God has used you, as well as others, to lead me back to Him. I am a different person today. Thank you for your faithfulness to share what God has done in your life and what He has shown you.

God Bless You,
Martha N_____

Dear Brother and Sister Wheeler,

I have just returned from the convention this year very encouraged. I could go on and on but let me say this . . . Brother Wheeler, the last time you were in Ohio for the convention was the first time that I had ever sat under you as a minister, and let me say you were a powerful light to me. As we prepared to come to convention this year I was hoping that you had not changed in your ministering humble spirit. I was thrilled that you had not changed in any way for the worse but that you had grown and shine an even brighter light. My husband could not come with me for the first convention and I have been going on and on about "Little Bear" for the last several years. When we heard you'd be there this year we began making plans to come. I am so glad we did. Another couple came with us and they enjoyed you as well. Your ministry is powerful and your spirit is the most sincere and humble I have ever known. I give all the glory to God for making you in His image. I wish not to exalt you, for I wish not to see you abased. However, I do wish to give you honor as surely it is due. It is my honor to know you and I would very much like to invite you here but our church is small and I am not sure how to go about it with the promotion. But, if the

Lord wills and you are anywhere near my area, I will if at all possible pack my family and bring them to hear words of encouragement in a time when they are so needed. We are very limited in our income, but it is my sincere desire to order something from you every month and build our own collection. I, too, collect Elsie Dinsmore books and have found a bookstore in my hometown which gets access to them through used book sales and I have many of the originals. Bless you and yours as you endeavor to serve Jesus. God bless you—Amen and Amen.

In Christ's Abundant Love,
Beverly C_____

Well, my friend, I thank you for reading this story, which was written with a sincere desire to give honor and praise to my Father in Heaven and my Lord and Savior Jesus Christ. By the grace of God and until the passing of time and events, I will add to the words of this autobiography. If it does not please the Lord for me to do so, then my hope is to meet you again—*HERE, THERE,* or in the *AIR!*

"For if we believe that Jesus died and rose again, even so them also which sleep in Jesus will God bring with Him. For this we say unto you by the Word of the Lord, that we which are alive and remain unto the coming of the Lord shall not prevent them which are asleep. For the Lord Himself shall descend from heaven with a shout, with the voice of the archangel, and with the trump of God: and the dead in Christ shall rise first: Then we which are alive and remain shall be caught up together with them in the clouds, to meet the Lord in the air: and so shall we ever be with the Lord. Wherefore comfort one another with these words" (I Thessalonians 4:14-18).

SPECIAL THANKS

"No man is an Island, entire of itself;" .....
John Donne (1571-1631)

This is a true statement. Indeed, my life's story is made up of numerous people the Lord brought into my life at times to help mold and shape my character. Below are many in alphabetical order. If I have neglected to list you, please do not hold it against me. Time has a way of causing lapses of the mind. God knows who you are, and may He reward you all for what you have done for me over the seasons of times you had in my life. Many have prayed for my ministry which I am unaware of and will never be able to personally thank this side of heaven.

First of all, my precious wife, Marilyn,
our daughters, Noelle and Aimee,
and our son, Joshua.

Also:

Sue Adams-Friend
The Jack Basey Family-Friends
The Kevin Bee Family-Friends
Earl Brent-Vocal Coach/Friend
The Richard Burkett Family-Friends
The Bob Clark Family-In-laws
The Jim Class Family-Friends
The Robert Cobb Family-In-laws
Abbe Hill Cromes-Friend/secretary
The Bill Counts Family-Seminary Bible teacher
Billy Davis-Friend since junior high school
Fred Deaver-Royal Ranger Leader/artist
The Gary Doran Family-Friends
The Mike Disbrow Family-Friends

Keith Elder-Pastor
The Egloff Family-Friends
The Craig Englert Family-Friends
The Marshall Foster Family-Friends
The Mike Gwinn Family-Friends
The Ronny Gilmore Family-Pastor/friends
The Bob Hall Family-Friends
The Mike Hodges Family-Pastor/friends
The Joe Johnson Family-Friends
The Bob Karlin Family-Friends
The Mike Kiley Family-Pastor/friend
Bob and Kathy Likes-Friends
Hal Lindsey-Bible Teacher/friend
Al and Mary Nevarez-Cousin
The Gustavo Nelson Family-Uncle
The Dr. Jim Leininger Family-Friends
Elis Wheeler Lessard-Sister
Anna Wheeler Lynd-Sister
Elizabeth Lobato Wheeler-Mother
Sylvia Lobato Henry-Sister
Mr. La Duke-Seventh-grade teacher
Richard Marriott-Friend/Royal Ranger leader
Peter Marshall-Author/friend
The Al Mendenhall Family-Friends
The Don Miller Family-Friends
The Linus Morris Family-Bible Teacher/friend
The Ruben Pizarro, Family-Friends
The Gavino Perez Family-Friends
Evangelist Dave Roever
The John Patterson Family-Friends
The Bob Patterson Family-Friends
The Keith Payne Family-Friends
Mark Pellet-Friend
The Doug Phillips Family-Friends
The Steve Phillips Family-Friends

Dick Prewitt-Friend
Ed Rasmussen-Pastor
The Sal Ruocco Family-Friends
The Ted Stanford Family-Friends
The Jeff Sandersier Family-Friends
The Ferd Staffel Family-Friends
Bruce Staffel Family-Friends
Bob Tope-Friend
The Bob Unruh Family-Pastor/friend
The Robert Welch Family-Friends
The Richard Welch Family-Friends
Mr. Welch-Sixth-grade teacher
Pat & Sue Welch-Editors of The Teaching Home magazine
Joseph Wheeler-Stepfather
Jack Wheeler-Great step uncle
The Bob Wilson Family-Friends
The Dwight Young Family-Friends

And to the rest of you who are yet to make your appearance in my like known only in the counsels of God, my Father, Jesus my Savior, Holy Spirit, my Guide.

* Thanks to numerous pastors who have shared their pulpits for church services. Camp coordinators, and all the National Homeschool leaders who have allowed our ministry to be a part of the Homeschool Community in their states.

* Extra special thanks to chief editors Mrs. Viola Moss, Karen Weber, and Mrs. Harriett Leddy who spent untold hours editing this book. Without them this book would not likely be a reality. Also thanks to Tamara Willey, Amber Brannon, Mary Minich, Abbe Hill Cromes-Friend/secretary all were readers and editors.

* Special thanks to Al Mendenhall Graphics for cover design and the Stonewall Valley Ranch, Fredricksberg, Texas for allowing me the setting for photos.

LITTLE BEAR'S

PHOTO

ALBUM

My mother as a Carmelite nun in
Mexico City

My dad Richard, mother Betty,
sister Sylvia and baby Richard
Los Angeles, California 1948

Graduation from Little Mayflower
Catholic Kindergarten 1953

"Little Bear" in the making 1953

"Little Bear" the making 1950

This was the age that I realized that
I could not write, read, or spell.
Lockwood Valley, California, age 9, 1957

My step-great Uncle Jack Wheeler,
WW I veteran, pioneered 160 acres i
Lockwood Valley just after the war

While living in this cabin in the winter, we
had no heat except from the old wood stove.
I remember waking up in this primitive cabin
to temperatures of less than 20 degrees at times.

Sisters Sylvia, Elizabeth, mother, and m
while living in Lockwood valley,
California, in 1957.

My sister Elizabeth and myself while living
in Lockwood Valley, California, 1957.

My sister Elizabeth and myself while li
in Lockwood Valley, California, in 19
I was downright proud that I could ge
shoot my uncle Jack's 22 rifle.

(Left to right) Bart Pellet, me,
and Mark Pellet 1962

Mark Pellet
Lockwood Valley, California 1962

Billy Davis
Santa Monica, California 1961

Mark Pellet and I camping in
Lockwood Valley, California 1964

(Left to right) Randy Como, me, Mr. and
rs. Como, Randy's cousin. Randy innocently
ed to kill me by offering me the drug of LSD.
He died in 1965 in Santa Monica, California
of a drug overdose

Played city baseball and discovered I did
not like team sports.
Took up surfing instead.

Surfing was good exercise.
Santa Monica, California 1967

Marilyn, girl of my dreams 1968 the year I met her

Marilyn's High School Graduation 1970

Marilyn and I were married
July 29, 1972

Wedding party (left to right)
Mr. And Mrs. Cobb, Marilyn and
my mother and step-father

Newborn Noelle
September 27, 1976

Newborn Aimee
June 3, 1980

Newborn Joshu
March 17, 198

Earl Brent, my vocal coach 1970

Fess Parker (Davy Crockett) and me 1996

Bob and Carol Karlin. Carol was
Marilyn's college teacher that the
Lord used along with Tru Mullenholf
in March of 1972 to lead us to Christ

The Bible Seminary I entered in 1973. Today many students and teachers are
in full time ministry. In picture are teachers Dallas Pastor Bill Counts,
Hawaiian Pastor Greg Englert, Pastor Tom Brewer, missionary Linus Morris,
Evangelist Marshall Foster, and Authors Hal Lindsay and John Weldon

Port Orford Harbor 1978
It was on a salmon fishing boat like these
that I spent my summer salmon fishing.

Fishing was hard work
I was always glad to
be home with my famil

Deep sea fishing with Capt. Dick Burkett

Friend Steve Phillips.
It was Steve that fired
me and encouraged me
to seek the Lord about
full-time ministry

Our first home needed a lot of fixing
By the time we were through it was j
fine. It was really just a shack.

Some of the children I ministered
to as a youth pastor

Battle Rock, Port Orford, Oregon 1
It was here on the backside of this
that I spent an hour in prayer and was
by the Lord into full time ministr

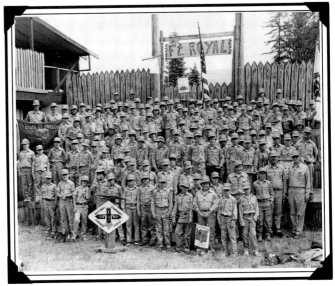

I Joined the Royal Rangers boys camping program in 1978,
little realizing that the Lord was going to use this ministry
to launch me into a national ministry

This was my Royal Ranger dress uniform

This was my Royal Ranger
Frontier Camping Fraternity dress
uniform. From this ministry
I received the name "Little Bear"
Which has followed me for 20 years.

Summer Stock at the
Pink Garter Theater in
Jackson, Wyoming 1971

Played the part of
Capt. Blaintree

Summer Stock at the
Pink Garter Theater in Jackson, Wyoming

Summer Stock at the Pink G
Theater in Jackson, Wyomir
Although I played the leadir
I did not care to associate m
the cast. Looking back I car
the Lord used all the acting
singing experiences for use
ministry today.

Misc Ministry Pictures